THE LIVING CHRIST

Conversation with a Teacher of Love

PAUL FERRINI

Book Design by Paul Ferrini
and Lisa Carta

Cover Art: Christ in the House of Martha and Mary
by Jan Vermeer, 1655, Oil on Canvas
used by permission of
the National Gallery of Scotland, Edinburgh

Library of Congress Number
2001094508

ISBN # 1-879159-49-X

Heartways Press
P.O. Box 99, Greenfield MA 01302

Manufactured in the United States of America

TABLE OF CONTENTS

Author's Preface

Part One

Part Two

Part Three

Author's Postscript

Appendix

To the indwelling Oneness
opening our hearts and minds
to love and truth
in this moment.

Author's Preface

About fifteen years ago, I began hearing a voice that kept saying "I want you to acknowledge me." I had been teaching *A Course in Miracles* at the time, but felt very uncomfortable telling people that the material came from Jesus. I didn't want to be thought of as some kind of Bible-thumping Christian, especially since my background was quite the opposite of that.

Raised as an Atheist with an appreciation for intellectual inquiry, I was drawn to *A Course in Miracles* because of its intellectual beauty and sophistication. The *Course* seemed to go beyond any kind of literal reading of the gospels to uncover the essential teachings of Jesus. It also put those teachings into a conceptual framework which had real psychological insight and was consistent within itself. For the first time, it seemed to me that the simple heart-centered teachings of the New Testament had been given a philosophical underpinning worthy of their lyricism and symbolic power.

As a result of working with this material and gathering respect for it, I was attuning more and more to the spirit of Jesus. Without knowing it, I had begun to cultivate a relationship with him. He had become the friend, the confidant, the other half of an inner dialogue with a teaching that had begun to resonate deeply in my cells.

So when I heard the voice saying "I want you to acknowledge me," the identity of the one speaking was never in doubt. Still, I withheld that acknowledgement for a very long time. I had to get comfortable with the idea of having a relationship with someone who was not in a body, someone whom others viewed as a God. And I had to overcome my anger at Christianity for what it had become.

Eventually, I gave him what he was asking of me, and a bond was formed between us. That bond has enabled me to surrender to his teaching in a way that otherwise would not have been possible. And it has helped me to become a spokesperson and a mouthpiece for the teaching in my own unique way.

A number of books followed. The first—*Love Without Conditions*—gradually became a best seller. The others—*The Silence of the Heart, Miracle of Love,* and *Return to the Garden*—built on that success. Many people felt that for the first time Jesus was speaking to them in a way that they could understand.

It has been a joy and an honor to be an instrument through which the teachings of this great soul could be offered to others in a way that speaks to their hearts. It is ecstatic work. And it is work that many of us are called to. When we accept a teaching and internalize it, we too become a vehicle through which that teaching expresses. Many of you who are reading these words will pass these empowering concepts on to others in your own unique way. That is the beauty of this ministry.

The present book departs somewhat from the format of the previous four *Christ Mind* books in that it is written in a question and answer format. The first two sections of this book consist of general questions to Jesus regarding subjects of interest to me, as well as personal questions relating to intimate relationships, work, and parenting. I hope that the exchanges with my teacher on these personal topics will make it clear that we all face similar challenges as we learn to align more fully with love in our lives.

The third section of this book contains questions posed by readers of my books. These questions were initially answered by me on my website. They have since been edited for publication and names have been changed to protect the privacy of the questioners.

These heartfelt questions help us to grasp some of the deeper challenges that face us as we endeavor to bring the power of Spirit into our daily lives. I hope that the answers I have given to these questions offer practical suggestions for integrating the teachings of Jesus into our lives.

Together the three parts of this book address what it means to give birth and expression to our Christ potential. We see what it means to face our fears and overcome our prejudices and narrow mindedness. The teachings of Jesus have very little to do with being perfect or mistake free and everything to do with accepting our imperfections and learning from our mistakes.

Problems and challenges face us every day of our lives. One of the great aspects of the Christ teaching is its practicality. There is no area of life that cannot be looked at through the eyes of love and transformed into an opportunity to learn and to grow.

Clearly, in the aftermath of the recent terrorist attacks on New York City and Washington, there is no better time to be looking for love in the depths of our hearts and souls. It is not easy to connect with love when we are hurt and afraid. But we have no choice if we want to heal and move on. Toward that end, I have included in the Appendix a poem that I wrote on the National Day of Mourning for the victims of these attacks. This poem celebrates the unselfish actions of many of our citizens and calls the people of our country to our highest and best response.

It is my hope that the contents of this book may help you bring understanding and compassion to yourself and to others.

I bow to the Christ Spirit Within you.

Paul Ferrini

Part One

Questions for Jesus

SUFFERING IS SELF CREATED

Paul: Many people have asked, and I among them, why me? Why did you come into my life and insist that we have a relationship.

Jesus: I'm sure that it appears that way to you. But I was already in your life. You just didn't know it. I had to remind you of why you were here, so you wouldn't go to sleep and forget your assignment.

Paul: What assignment do you mean?

Jesus: Well, everybody who embodies has a simple assignment: to open more deeply to the presence of love. That involves different things for different people. For you, it meant acknowledging that there was a spiritual presence available to you. You were on the edge for a while, you know.

Paul: I know. I didn't really want to be here. There was so much suffering. I didn't see the point to it.

Jesus: You aren't the only one who doesn't see the point. But you have come to learn over the years that a great deal of that suffering is self-created. It is not thrust upon you by some outside force or authority. You reach out and bring it in.

Paul: I know that when I am feeling unloved, I perceive the world in a very different way than when I am feeling loved!

Jesus: That's right. It's very much about perception. And perception is not just an intellectual affair. It includes what you think and how you feel about it.

17

Paul: So, would you say that we are here to alter our perception?

Jesus: You are here to perceive things as they are. You are here to learn that you create suffering by insisting on seeing the world in terms of what you want it to be or what you don't want it to be.

Paul: Are we here to learn how to be neutral? Not opposed or against?

Jesus: Yes, but neutral isn't the right word. You are here to understand thoroughly, intricately, how you create your own suffering by wanting something to be different than it is. And, as a byproduct of this learning, you stop having so many fixed ideas or opinions. You learn to let things be.

Paul: This seems to be a major component not only of your teaching, but of many spiritual teachings.

Jesus : Yes, it is one of the few central ideas on which enlightenment rests.

Paul: Can you elaborate?

Jesus : When you can let things be as they are, you stop wasting your time and your energy on external factors that you can do nothing about. Instead, you begin to wipe clean the glass that separates your self-concept from your true identity. In other words, you begin to see who you really are.

THINKING LIMITS BEING

Paul: So I am not who I think I am?

Jesus: Absolutely not. If you will sit in silence for just one minute, you will see that you are much greater than any thought you have about yourself. Every single thought limits you or someone else. And you are not limited, nor is anyone else.

Paul: So all our thoughts do is limit us?

Jesus: All thinking is a form of Self-conscription. Thinking limits being. Being is always larger than thinking. Truth is always larger and more immediate than the concepts we have about it.

Paul: So why do we think?

Jesus: You might as well have asked "Why do we incarnate?" Incarnation is also Self-conscription. It takes the vast, all encompassing Self and makes it particular. Now we don't just have Self, we have Paul or Jesus.

Paul: So Self is larger than Paul or Jesus?

Jesus: Self is Paul and Jesus remembering their true nature, remembering that they cannot be described by name or form. The true Paul or Jesus are beyond all thinking, beyond all concepts.

Paul: That seems so baffling!

Jesus: Exactly. It is beyond the ability of your mind to grasp it. It is the mystery. It is the awe we experience when we approach the throne of the All-Inclusive Oneness we call God.

Paul: The part does not know itself separate from the whole?

Jesus: Yes. When you become whole, there is no more part. There is no more you that is separate from anyone else.

Paul: Is that what your experience is?

Jesus: Yes, I am not separate from you or anyone else. When you think of Jesus, he is there instantly, not because he is a separate being you call upon, but because he and you were never separated.

Paul: I don't totally get it.

Jesus: Before embodiment there was no Jesus or Paul, but there was this mutual communion in the truth. Now, even though Jesus is not embodied, that communion in the truth continues.

CHANNELING

Paul: Well, this brings up the subject of channeling. I have been careful not to call what I do channeling. When Jesus and Paul have "communion in the truth," and I hear your words coming through me, is that channeling?

Jesus: How do you know they are my words and not yours?

Paul: Well, I don't really know. But I feel all this energy in my heart when I do this work and I sense your presence.

Jesus: How do you know it is my presence and not yours?

Paul: I don't really know this. I do know that it is a heightened state of consciousness, both thought and feeling.

Jesus: Yes, but that state of consciousness could come simply through your remembrance of who you are.

Paul: Yes, I guess that it could.

Jesus: There is nothing special about it.

Paul: Yes, that's why I don't want to call it channeling.

Jesus: Other people could do what you do. They could remember their true nature and they would experience this heightened state of consciousness. Right?

Paul: Yes.

Jesus: And in that state of consciousness you are in communion with the universal truth as well as with any specific expression of it you resonate with. If you resonate with Buddhism, you would be in communion with Buddha or with other teachers within that tradition.

Paul: So I am in communion with you because I resonate to your teachings?

Jesus: Yes, although I had to remind you of that fact.

Paul: Of course you are aware that I despised the Christian tradition because of all the bloodshed and oppression that has been committed in its name.

Jesus: Yes, and like most Jews, you were obsessed with suffering: your suffering and that of others in the world. You were addressed initially at this level.

Paul: So you were the one who sent me the Buber book when I was feeling suicidal? And you were the one who brought *A Course in Miracles* into my life.

Jesus: Well, it does not matter who brought these books to you. You asked and your call was answered. There is no illusion of separateness where I am. We work together energetically. We go wherever our unique energies can be helpful.

Paul: This is very confusing.

Jesus: I know. It is beyond your ability to grasp, yet you keep trying to grasp it.

JESUS AND PAUL

Paul: So what about this notion of channeling?

Jesus: Anyone who is sincere and committed can connect with higher energies, but no one can speak for anyone else.

Paul: So I cannot speak for you?

Jesus: No, but you and I can be in communion as you speak. Leave it to others to judge whether the words and energy you bring through feel like the words and energy of Jesus.

Paul: What is the difference between Paul remembering who

he is and speaking from that place and Jesus speaking through Paul?

Jesus: Well, it would be hard for Jesus to speak through Paul because there is no more Jesus.

Paul: No more Jesus?

Jesus: Remember the Jesus who was embodied once is no longer. You cannot hold this consciousness to where it was then.

Paul: But weren't you already free of limitation, before you even left your body?

Jesus: No one is free of limitation, even after leaving the body. The physical body is only one of many bodies. Every thought or feeling is a form of limitation.

Paul: So you have not finished your spiritual evolution?

Jesus: I know this sounds absurd to you, my friend, but even God has not finished!

Paul: Sometimes I think you take a perverse pleasure in confusing me. Do you stay up late trying to come up with new ways to push my buttons?

Jesus: Actually, your buttons aren't all that hard to push!

Paul: Oh, I see. Thanks a lot . . . .

Jesus: Seriously. This is not a timeline with a beginning or an end. It is a circular journey of awakening. We keep going around and around until we become completely conscious of who we are.

Paul: Is God completely conscious?

Jesus: God is completely loving, but not completely conscious.

Paul: How is this possible?

Jesus: If God were completely conscious there would be no expression of God: no you, no me, no world.

Paul: So when we all wake up the universe disappears?

Jesus: You could say that. But don't start counting the days . . . .

THE MILLENNIUM

Paul: What about millennium fever? Many people think that the world is going to end soon. Some Christians believe that you will be coming back to earth for the judgment day.

Jesus: Well, one year is no more final than any other. The universe could cease to be on any given day, but it isn't very likely. Every millennium has millennium fever. It's just your way of trying to make the time in which you live special.

Paul: So we don't have to worry about us human beings on planet earth blowing ourselves up or perishing in some ecological disaster?

Jesus: You can worry if you want, but worry won't help you avoid it if it comes.

Paul: I thought you said it won't come.

Jesus: Nobody knows whether it will come or whether it won't. I don't think the physical universe will end any time soon, but planet earth is still up for grabs.

Paul: Are there things that we should be doing to avoid a planetary disaster?

Jesus: Try loving one another and loving the planet you live on. Slow down a bit and take a deep breath. Find out what's really important and make that your priority. What would you do if today were your last day on planet earth? Would you go to work or stay home with your family?

Paul: Is it that simple?

Jesus: The concept is that simple. Implementing it might be somewhat challenging, but it would be well worth it.

Paul: Is it possible that the Kingdom of God can ever be present on earth?

Jesus: The possibility that this promise can be fulfilled is just as great as the possibility that it won't be.

Paul: So it depends on us?

Jesus: It depends on you individually and collectively. You are all responsible for the choices you make. You will reap what you have sown alone and together.

THE PAIN OF ATTACHMENT

Paul: Some years ago I left my marriage of fifteen years and began exploring new aspects of sharing and intimacy with other partners. Although these relationships provided many important learning experiences for me, I have been sad to see them end. Sometimes I wonder if I want to keep opening my heart if it means more beginnings and endings.

Jesus: Do you have any choice? Do you choose to open your heart or not open your heart?

Paul: I suppose not.

Jesus: So you will keep doing it. It will happen when it happens and there is nothing that you can do about it. What would you like to do differently?

Paul: I would like to open up when it is truly mutual and there is sufficient compatibility to support a lifetime partnership.

Jesus: So if you meet someone who is not ready and your heart opens, what will you do?

Paul: Well, that just happened. She wasn't free to commit to the relationship, so I told her I had to back off.

Jesus: Is your heart still open?

Paul: Well, I had to detach and it was very difficult. I was so emotionally attached to her. I would say that my heart is still open, but I am afraid to see her. I don't want to get re-attached.

Jesus: You can see that the pain lies in the attachment.

Attachment may seem okay as long you stay together, but when you and the other person decide to part ways, the attachment becomes painful. You labor under the misconception that you need this person and cannot live without her. That is not true. That is an idea that keeps you a prisoner.

Paul: In the initial stages of detachment, I felt as if I was dying. I wasn't even sure if I wanted to live without her.

Jesus: You were dying, but not very gracefully I'm afraid!

Paul: I know. I was still trying to hold onto her. I had to stop expecting anything from her. I had to come to terms with the distinct possibility that she would no longer be in my life.

Jesus: So, now that you have done that, you are no longer attached, correct?

Paul: Yes, that's true.

Jesus: So your heart is open and yet you are not attached. Isn't that an improvement over what you had before?

Paul: Yes, it is.

COMMITMENT

Paul: How important is commitment in a relationship?

Jesus: Commitment is essential in a relationship. The greater the commitment, the more potential for psychological and spiritual growth.

Paul: Can you say a little more about this?

Jesus: Commitment means that you intend to love and appreciate this person. It means that you are willing to look at your fears and insecurities so that they don't undermine the relationship. It means that you are willing to forgive yourself and the other person when you make mistakes. It means that you are willing to listen to each other, even when you feel unloved and unappreciated. It means that you accept the daily challenge of the relationship as a spiritual practice. You keep trusting your life together as it unfolds. Each day you renew your commitment.

Paul: It sounds like you are describing a spiritual marriage or partnership.

Jesus: Yes. That is what it is. But it is not for everybody.

Paul: And that is because. . . ?

Jesus: Because some people are not ready to make this kind of commitment to each other, so they make lesser commitments and this is fine too. It's important for people to be realistic about what they can commit to and not to make promises they can't keep. It is better to make a small commitment you can keep than to make a larger one you can't keep.

Paul: Do people need to make small commitments before they make larger ones?

Jesus: This is one way to do it. It is a good way to test the relationship to see how strong it is. But not everyone has to do this. When two people are ripe, emotionally available and come together in a mutually respectful and trusting way, commitment can be instantaneous. Both people know right away.

Paul: That's what I thought happened with _____.

Jesus: Yes, but she was not ready for this commitment. Only she knows why this is the case. It certainly has nothing to do with you.

Paul: I know. . . . That's part of the sadness I feel.

Jesus: It goes with the territory. People do not always know what they want or what they need. And so they make promises they cannot keep.

FORGIVENESS 101

Paul: When people treat each other unkindly, does this create some kind of relationship karma?

Jesus: Everything you do to someone else will be done to you; if not now, at some other time.

Paul: That is an awesome statement.

Jesus: Yes, it is. When you act in a way that is hurtful to another, you must in some way feel the pain that you caused. Feeling that pain enables you to experience compassion for the other person and, ultimately for yourself.

When you feel compassion, you want to ask forgiveness for any pain you have caused. You want make amends to the person you have hurt.

Without compassion for yourself and others, true forgiveness is not possible.

Paul: If compassion and forgiveness are so important, why don't we teach these subjects in our schools?

Jesus: That's a good question. You might as well understand once and for all that being in a relationship without knowing how to forgive yourself and the other person is like being in a river without knowing how to swim.

Paul: It's hopeless?

Jesus: It can work only when the river is calm. As soon as the wind starts to blow and the current picks up, swimming skills are necessary.

Paul: You are painting a rather grim picture.

Jesus: It isn't really grim. It's just realistic. You might have good weather for a week or two, but how long can you expect it to last? Sooner or later, it's going to rain. . . . You don't go into a relationship unless you know you can weather the storm together.

Paul: So we have to know our partners fairly well before getting into a committed relationship, right?

Jesus: You have to know that your partner can swim before you go swimming with him or her, do you not? Think about it. Would you jump into the water with your partner if you knew s/he couldn't swim? Are you prepared to save not only yourself, but your partner too? Do you know how to deal with a drowning person without being pulled down yourself? Are your lifesaving skills that good?

Paul: I guess that Forgiveness 101 is a required course. You have to take it before you take Relationship 101.

Jesus: I think they are the same course! You don't learn how to forgive in a vacuum. You learn in relationship with others. But it's an entry level course to be sure. You don't take Relationship 301 until you take Relationship 101.

Paul: In other words you don't promise to marry someone until you know that you can live with that person?

Jesus: That's right. You find out if you have the skillfulness to live together. You find out if you enjoy similar interests and values. You find out if you are both ready to take the plunge. And I assure you it is a plunge!

THE PATH OF THE HEART

Paul: When we are attracted to someone, it's easy to get emotionally involved with that person, but it's not so easy to become emotionally dis-entangled if it doesn't work out. You jump in with your heart and your head doesn't have any choice. But you try to get out with your head and your heart doesn't always cooperate.

Jesus: That's the classic conflict. Your heart doesn't stop loving. But your mind helps you realize that some relationships are a one way street. You keep moving forward, but the person facing you keeps receding.

Paul: Which is another way of saying "you can't love someone who is not there."

Jesus: Well, you can love that person, but s/he might not love you back! So if you are looking for a mutual commitment, a love dance, it might be in your best interest to let that person go.

Sometimes, we learn a lot about love by releasing someone who is not ready to commit to us. It can be painful, but we come out of the experience stronger, because we have not compromised ourselves.

Paul: That's why I got response #202 (*The Fire of Change*) when I consulted *The Way of Peace* oracle about _____. It told me that I'd get over the pain and come out stronger.

Jesus: That's what happens when you face change bravely. When you see that there is no escape from the flames, you walk right into them. It may hurt, but the pain is quickly over. If you hold onto someone who isn't ready to commit, the pain lingers without changing the outcome. Sooner or later you will have to let go. You will have to say goodbye and mourn the loss.

Paul: I guess that's what it means to be on the Path of the Heart.

Jesus: That's right. One whose heart is open doesn't deny his feelings. He moves through his feelings courageously with an uncanny trust in the process.

As you know, my teaching is not about avoiding experience, but about engaging experience at the deepest level. It is not a retreat from the world, but a willingness to be in the world without being caught in the illusory drama.

JUDAISM AND CHRISTIANITY 1

Paul: Yesterday was Yom Kippur, the Day of Atonement. Do you have anything to say about this Jewish holy day?

Jesus: This holy day is about endings and beginnings. In order to begin something new, we need to let go of the old. Then, we can begin with a clean slate. We forgive the past and move on with renewed vision and hope. However, celebrating Yom Kippur once a year is not enough. Each day must be Yom Kippur.

Paul: You are a hard taskmaster!

Jesus: Not as hard as you think. When you forgive and let go of the past on a daily basis, it's not so hard to do. But when you wait a full year, it's excruciating work. I ask people to lighten their load a little each day. Otherwise, when Rosh Hashanah comes, they are like Atlas holding up the world.

Paul: Do you still consider yourself a Jew?

Jesus: Well, my mission was to bring Judaism back to its Source so that it could be a universal teaching. That meant that a lot of unnecessary dogma and tradition had to be challenged. As you know, it wasn't a very popular mission!

Paul: Is Christianity any more true to your teaching than Judaism was to the teaching of Moses?

Jesus: No. In some ways it has gone even further astray. But there are individuals who understand.

Paul: That seems to be the case, no matter what religion we are talking about, is it not?

Jesus: Yes. Religion is the outer shell. The seed of truth must break through the shell if it is going to bear fruit. Each person must find faith within before s/he can be a witness for it. When the shell is hollow—just a profession of rote beliefs and mindless rituals—people have a right to reject it. No one should accept a teaching unless it resonates in his heart and his mind.

Paul: So you don't believe that questioning authority is such a bad thing?

Jesus: I don't know why you are even asking me that question. All I have ever done is to question authority, and I encourage everyone else to do so! Don't take someone else's word for it. Find out for yourself. Truth is in your heart. It can be reflected in the teachings of others, but that is not its source. Its source is always internal.

KARMA AND REINCARNATION

Paul: There's another subject that should be addressed here and that is reincarnation. Is there such a thing?

Jesus: Reincarnation, as you picture it, does not occur. You don't come back in a human body, nor do you come back as a cow or an ant. Your soul has many dimensions of experience where learning continues to happen and consciousness continues to develop.

Paul: So all those incarnations of the Buddha aren't for real, and there will be no Second Coming?

Jesus: Well, Buddha is not a person but a state of awareness. Anyone can become a Buddha, just as anyone can become a Christ, simply by realizing his/her true nature. Of course, it doesn't happen very often, but often enough that the idea that there is only one Buddha or Christ is ludicrous!

Paul: So Jesus will not come again. Gautama will not come again.

Jesus: That's right. But they have not ceased to exist. We continue to demonstrate truth to all who are attuned to us and to our teachings.

Paul: What about the law of karma? Is there such a thing?

Jesus: Yes, as you sow, so do you reap. The energy that you put out eventually returns to you. Your chickens come home to roost.

You cannot judge or attack another person without judging and attacking yourself. Life is a mirror. The person you love or hate is just a reflection of yourself.

Paul: So there is no escape from the boomerang effect of our thoughts and actions?

Jesus: That's right. There is no escape. You have to come to terms with everything you think, feel or do.

Paul: If we don't come to terms with it, are we punished?

Jesus: There is no punishment, except perhaps for the fact that you must continue in the same classroom with the same or a similar teacher and similar companions. You don't move on.

Paul: So it's a living hell. We continue to be bored, depressed, reactive. But we don't roast in the flames?

Jesus: No, the flames are symbolic. You must live with your own consciousness until you change it. That's the only hell there is. But the pain of this is not to be underestimated!

Paul: "No Exit," huh? I guess Jean Paul Sartre was onto something.

Jesus: Yes, he understood the nature of psychological pain and the prison that each person lives in.

Paul: Well, it's a relief to know that hell is of our own making and that you are not going to judge us harshly.

Jesus: Why would I put myself in a position to judge you when I know that any judgment I have about anyone is a judgment about myself? My ease and peace of mind can only be maintained so long as I hold you innocent.

LOVING YOUR ENEMY

Paul: Can you see the innocence of people like Charles Manson, Ted Bundy, or Adolph Hitler?

Jesus: If I could not do it for them, I could not do it for you or for myself. There are no exceptions to the law of love.

Paul: What is the law of love?

Jesus: Love expresses as acceptance, non-judgment and compassion. Anything other than this is not love. It is fear. You can call it love, but it is not love.

Paul: Why is it important that we see our own dark side?

Jesus: If you can't see your own dark side—your fear with all its personifications—you won't be able to feel compassion for others who are acting in unloving ways. You will judge others, not realizing that the very qualities you dislike in them are the ones you cannot accept in yourself. Your hatred of your enemy is merely the projection of your own self-hatred.

You can turn this around by accepting your dark side. When you understand how crazy fear can make you, you feel compassion for people who are in the grip of fear. You don't want to make them more afraid. You want them to realize that they are worthy of love and appreciation.

It is paradoxical, but when you accept your shadow, you become the light. You become the possibility of love where love seems impossible.

Paul: Your teaching is very psychological.

Jesus: I have always addressed the inner person, not the outer one. I am more interested in how someone thinks and feels than I am in what someone does. I have never been interested in changing behavior. I am interested in changing hearts. When the heart is changed, behavior changes by itself. Anything else is pure bribery. It tells the person "I'll give you two cookies if you're nice." It's conditional. The motivation to be nice ends when the cookies have been given out." It is not a real solution to the problem of suffering.

Paul: What is the real solution?

Jesus: Understand that you are capable of saying or doing what anyone says or does. Do not make that person into a scapegoat, but learn to love him. In loving him, you are loving the fearful, overwhelmed, imperfect aspect of yourself.

Every time you feel compassion for your enemy, you experience the most profound healing because you realize that there is no part of you that is unworthy of love and acceptance. Your enemy is therefore your greatest teacher. Touch his heart and your own is strengthened. It is better than a cookie, and less fattening!

TRUTH AND DISTORTION

Paul: You use a lot of stories and metaphors when you teach.

Jesus: Yes, without metaphors and stories I could not teach, nor could you.

Paul: Why is that?

Jesus: Because metaphors and stories paint a picture that is psychologically rich and emotionally engaging. They help people connect with the spirit of truth. Scripture without metaphor or story is too linear, too intellectual. It is misleading because it doesn't capture the dimension of the heart.

Paul: Yet so many passages in the Bible are misinterpreted

because people want to interpret them literally. Most people, for example, believe that Mary was a virgin, that you are the only Son of God, and that you were physically resurrected. They want to make you special.

Jesus: Supernatural powers are always attributed to the divine as a way of creating distance between the divine and the human. However, I am a bridge between the human and divine. I bring these two worlds together. I experience my humanity and my divinity together and invite you to do the same.

Unfortunately, many of you are threatened by that invitation. You are not ready to claim your divinity. You believe that you must be mistake-free to be a son or a daughter of God. I have told you that this is not true, but you do not believe me.

Those in power would keep your self-deception alive. They don't care if you worship me because I am dead and gone. But they certainly don't want to you imitate me and claim your divinity. They do not want you to acknowledge a higher law than the secular one that keeps them in power.

When I was in the body, those in power sought to take away my divinity by killing my humanity, but their plan backfired. Instead of making me go away, they made me into a martyr. Thanks to them, my divinity was strengthened and my humanity was forgotten.

It is ironic, but the very reason for my coming was thereby subverted. After I died, a religion was created in my name that taught the very principles I had come to undo!

Paul: It's amazing, is it not?

Jesus: Yes, it is the ultimate irony. It's easy being a savior when everyone is looking for salvation from someone else, but it isn't so easy to empower people to save themselves!

Paul: Why do we need to make you into a savior?

Jesus: It is the only way that you can come to terms with my death! Unless you endow me with supernatural powers, you can't take my teaching to heart. Are you going to say "Here's another poor schmuck who got crucified on the cross: let's follow him"? Of course not. You have to make me special. You have to say: "He could have stopped the crucifixion, but he didn't, because he knew that he would be resurrected. He knew that God was taking care of him."

In other words, "I was never in danger. I never felt any pain," and so forth. That's absurd and you know it, yet you believe it anyway because, in a way, it takes you off the hook . . . unless you're Jewish, that is.

JUDAISM AND CHRISTIANITY 2

Jesus: If you're Jewish, you're still on the hook, because guess who killed Christ? And don't tell me you don't know! Don't tell me that no one ever suggested that maybe you were to blame for my death?

My crucifixion meant freedom for Christians and death for Jews. It was the end of Judaism as we knew it and the beginning of a new idolatry.

Paul: So you consider Christians idolatrous?

Jesus: If they believe that I am the only son of God and that I died for their sins, then they are idolatrous! Instead of claiming their own salvation, they are trying to find it through me. That does not work. I cannot save anyone.

Paul: But you yourself have said "I am the Door."

Jesus: Yes, but there is a difference between being the door and being the Source. Anyone can be the door.

Paul: Yes, but many people want you to be the only door.

Jesus: If there was only one door, there would be a long line out in front of it. . . . I don't see any line, do you?

Paul: The only line I see is the one for the new Star Wars film.

Jesus: Well, at least I'm not the only idol!

Paul: That's right. We've made a little progress in these secular times.

You mentioned before that your death meant freedom for Christians and death for Jews. Can you elaborate?

Jesus: Christians got the strongest argument. They got the resurrection. They got the afterlife. They were willing to sacrifice a lot because of a promise of a better day. They had "right" and eventually "might" on their side.

Jews became scapegoats for every problem in the world. They were hunted and maimed and butchered. And eventually they lost their faith.

The "chosen" people were "chosen" for collective crucifixion. There are dangers involved in standing apart.

Had they listened to the teaching I brought, this might have been avoided. It was essentially a Jewish teaching. I spoke as a prophet and a messenger within that tradition. I brought the word of God as Moses and Abraham had done before me.

I simply asked them to give up one thing: their specialness.

Paul: What would have happened if the Jews had accepted you as a prophet?

Jesus: There would have been a complete renewal of the faith. And Judaism would have become a universal teaching, open to everyone. You would not have needed to be born Jewish to become a Jew. Plus, the rabbis would have stopped trying to prescribe endless rituals for people to perform and started to encourage people to look inside their hearts for answers. It would have become a vital, enlightened teaching.

Judaism lost a great deal by refusing to recognize my teaching. And Christianity could never gain what Judaism lost. It was a missed opportunity.

Paul: What about now? Don't Judaism and Christianity have the opportunity now to come into alignment with that teaching?

Jesus: Judaism would have to stop being Jewish and Christianity would have to stop being Christian and then the teaching could flower. It would take an atmosphere of great openness and respect for all points of view.

That is what is needed now: a movement beyond creeds and dogmas into the heart of truth. It is time for religions to recognize the moral and spiritual values they hold in common and emphasize these. Today there is a flowering of spirituality in the minds and hearts of the people. People are discovering the need for spiritual values at home and at work. They need churches and temples that meet them where they are. Religion must be relevant, indeed intimate with people. It must engage people at the deepest level and in the areas they care the most about.

Paul: So we must move beyond labels?

Jesus: Yes, the spirit of love, help, kindness, acceptance needs no label. It is known by its deeds and funded spontaneously by people who admire and support those deeds.

THE BIBLE

Paul: Wasn't a lot of the Christian teaching distorted in the push to export it?

Jesus: Yes. It's hard to take a teaching that is essentially revolutionary and make it palatable to masses of people without losing something important in the translation. Those who sought to give the teaching told their own version of it. You have their gospels not mine.

Paul: So what we know as the New Testament is not completely accurate?

Jesus: Of course it's not. You can tell just by reading it that passages are written by men who were in fear. What comes from fear is not, and cannot ever be, my teaching.

Paul: What part of your teaching is preserved in the bible?

Jesus: Do not judge your brothers and sisters. Love one

another. Even love your enemies. Whatever you do to the least of your brethren you do to me.

Paul: And just for the record, what was distorted?

Jesus: The idea that I was an only son of God and died for your sins, the virgin birth, the resurrection, the second coming and the times of tribulation. Revelation is one of the most distorted documents in the Bible. It relapses into the fire and brimstone rhetoric of the Old Testament: the idea that if you are not good, God will destroy the world. Why would a loving God do anything to harm his own Creation? If S/he were capable of intervening, would S/he not send help instead of punishment?

Paul: That's a good point. Some people believe that you were that help—that God gave his only begotten Son to us to help us and teach us. Is this just a story?

Jesus: I would like you to realize that it's all story. Some of the story orbits around the truth, and some of it spins out of orbit into many fearful directions. You need to learn to discriminate between the true stories and the false ones.

Paul: Well, many people think that the Bible is the one true story, and you seem to be challenging that idea.

Jesus: The Bible was the creation of many minds with many different experiences. There is great beauty and truth in it. Some of the stories about me are essentially true. They are embellished, as all stories are, but they capture the flavor of my life. But as soon as one fearful word is put in my mouth, a foothold is created for untruth. And there are those who would take advantage of the foothold to erect an elaborate edifice full of lies.

If you want to understand my teaching, read the Bible with a discriminating eye. Take everything into your heart and your experience and live it there. If it helps you open to love, then it is true. If not, it is false. This is the only way you can know the truth. Never take someone else's word for it, even mine. Even Mine!

Paul: So you want us to question your authority too?

Jesus: You must question everyone's authority. The only true authority is God and S/he is silent on many of the issues that separate one human being from another. But in that silence, the truth will be found, if you have the patience to be still and the courage to listen.

Paul: There are many people today who are preaching doom and gloom. Are they off-base?

Jesus: Well, they are living in their own ballpark with their own audience. Unfortunately, there's no team on the field. There's no one to cheer for.

Paul: Meaning what?

Jesus: Meaning that they are creating their own misery. They suffer not because the world is going to end, but because they think it's going to end. And because they are so focused on the future, they don't attend to what's right in front of them. They are giving up their power to create a meaningful life.

Paul: Isn't that the result of all fear-based thinking?

Jesus: Yes!

NOT BEING ASHAMED OF OUR FEARS

Paul: So everything that is stirred up by our fear is delusional?

Jesus: Yes. On the other hand, it is natural for you to have fears. You don't have to be ashamed of them. You don't have to hide them or pretend not to have them. You just have to see them for what they are!

Paul: And they are?

Jesus: They are illusions. They are untruth. They are your view of the world as a victim, as one who has no power to choose or to change. And that view is a fiction!

Paul: So our fear is a fiction?

Jesus: Well, it's like going to a movie and coming out and realizing that it was just a movie. It didn't really happen. But you believed it was happening while you were watching it. You had thoughts and feelings about it. You were afraid. You were anxious. You were involved in the drama.

Of course, it's okay that you got drawn into the movie. You aren't going to be punished. But it's over now and you can let it go. Next time, with a little more vigilance, you'll watch the movie without buying into it. You'll witness the drama, instead of participating in it.

Paul: You are talking about detachment, are you not? Are you perhaps a closet Buddhist?

Jesus: I hate to tell you this but I came out of the closet a long time ago!

HOMOSEXUALITY

Paul: You better watch out or there will be a line outside and there won't be many of us in it who are straight!

Jesus: As you know, it makes no difference to me what someone's sexual orientation is. Homosexuality is a perversion, but it is harmless if it happens in the context of a loving relationship. Anything can be transformed by the power of love and acceptance.

Paul: There are many gay people who would gag on your use of the word perversion.

Jesus: Well, anal sex and oral sex are perversions. It doesn't stop both men and women from engaging in these activities, nor does it make them "bad" if they do.

Paul: So it is not sinful?

Jesus: The only actions which are sinful are actions that hurt you or other people. And sinful does not mean "bad." It means wrong or untrue. It means that this action will lead to suffering.

Paul: It seems to be a very important point in your teaching that you can be wrong or mistaken without being "evil" or bad.

Jesus: That's right. Every one of you is mistaken, at least once an hour, if not more frequently. If mistakes made you "evil," there wouldn't be any "good" people out there. That is why I can say prostitution is perverse. It exploits people and leads to suffering. But I cannot condemn the prostitute. I can simply remind her that she has a choice. No matter what she chooses, she is worthy of my love.

Paul: In other words, "who will throw the first stone?"

Jesus: Yes. It is not for us to judge one another.

Paul: Then why call homosexuality a perversion? Doesn't that encourage people to view the homosexual as "bad."

Jesus: I am afraid that it might. And I don't want to say anything that would encourage that. When I use the word perversion, I simply mean that it "isn't natural." What is natural is for a man and woman to come together for the purpose of loving one another and raising a family.

Paul: Well, most of our sexuality isn't natural then. Because most people engage in sexual activity because it is enjoyable, not because they are trying to have children.

Jesus: That's true. And I would say that if love is present between those persons, then no harm is done. And if love is not present, then suffering will result.

Paul: So what matters most is not the activity per se— whether it is natural or perverse—but whether love is present. Is that what you are saying?

Jesus: Yes. That is what I am saying.

Paul: So you would not object to a gay or lesbian marriage?

Jesus: No, assuming that marriage is an act of love.

Paul: So if two people of the same sex live together in a loving, committed way and have sex together it is unnatural, but not harmful or wrong. Correct?

Jesus: That's right. It may even be a creation of great spiritual beauty if unconditional love is present between the partners!

Paul: So homosexuality is unnatural but not wrong. It might even be right?

Jesus: Yes, it might be an unnatural relationship that is very right because it is infused with love and tenderness. Remember, it is not the form that matters, but the content.

Paul: I think I'm beginning to understand your position. Let's try this out: say a man and a woman engage in anal sex without love. In your view, this would be both an unnatural act and a harmful one. Is that true?

Jesus: That is true.

Paul: But if they engage in the same act with love in their hearts, then the act is unnatural, but not harmful. Is that correct?

Jesus Yes, that is correct.

Paul: So what should the Church's official position on homosexuality be?

Jesus: It's a novel idea, to ask me what the Church's position should be. I haven't been asked such a question in a long time!

THE POPE, BIRTH CONTROL, ABORTION

Paul: Doesn't the Pope consult with you?

Jesus: Let's just say that he's doing the best that he can, but he doesn't realize that the content can completely spiritualize the form. For example, he doesn't understand that God can be deeply present in a homosexual union.

You have to remember that priests don't know very much about sexuality. They are the last people in the world that you should consult for a definition of healthy sexuality. If you want a definition of healthy sexuality, talk to couples who have been together for twenty years and still delight in each other's presence. Don't ask the Pope. He would be clueless.

Paul: Yet millions of people look to him for guidance on such issues.

Jesus: Yes, I know. It's not an issue that the Pope is knowledgeable about. All he has to rely on is the dogma of his church. That won't be helpful to people who are struggling with these issues.

Paul: So, just to carry this discussion to its natural conclusion. . . . You would say that birth control is unnatural but not necessarily wrong or harmful, yes?

Jesus: Yes. It is not harmful to prevent conception.

Paul: What about abortion?

Jesus: Abortion is both unnatural and harmful. It is hurtful not just to the baby, but also to the mother. It is in the true sense a barbarous act!

Paul: What about those on the Christian Right who take the life of doctors who perform abortions?

Jesus: They are misguided souls. You never win hearts by taking lives. The only way that abortion can be prevented is for those who are against abortion to act in loving ways toward women who are having abortions and their doctors. Offer alternatives to abortion, like adoption programs where the expenses of mothers are paid and babies are placed with parents who want them. But be sure to offer the woman the choice to keep her child if she changes her mind. And give her the support services she needs to raise that child. Then, fewer and fewer people will want to have abortions.

Don't try to hurt or punish people who are in favor of abortion. That will only increase their determination to oppose you. And you are not the issue. The baby is the issue. Offer pregnant women incentives to give birth to their babies. Offer them a loving community to belong to. Offer them counseling and information on birth control so that they do not have unwanted pregnancies. Be a minister of love and comfort, not an accuser, a judge, or an executioner.

To be against abortion is not enough. You must find out what you are for! Be for choices and those who are pro-choice will begin to listen. Then this unfortunate conflict will die down, and a new era of understanding and tolerance will be born.

Paul: You are always on the side of love!

Jesus: That's right. If you ever see it otherwise, then I want you to challenge me.

GUIDED BY THE LAW OF LOVE

Paul: Okay. So back now to the question about the Church's position on homosexuality. What should it be?

Jesus: All religious organizations must be guided by the law of love. They must sanction loving unions, no matter what they look like. They must support people who are willing to commit themselves to living and learning together.

Paul: Even if those unions involve unnatural acts?

Jesus: The Church does not have to come out and say that homosexuality is good or that it is natural. It doesn't need to have an opinion about the lifestyle choices people make. Its only requirement should be that people love each other and be prepared to go through all the ups and downs of life together. The Church must advocate spiritual partnership between people and then give people the freedom to make their own choices.

Paul: What about people who don't want to be legally married?

Jesus: A legal marriage may or may not be a spiritual partnership. As long as the partnership is sincere, it doesn't matter whether or not the state recognizes it.

Paul: And the same is true for divorce?

Jesus: Yes, marriage or partnership is a mutual commitment. Divorce is the absence of a mutual commitment.

Paul: Isn't it helpful to have a public ceremony, in which the intentions of the partners are witnessed by their friends and family members? Doesn't that help to make the commitment real for both people?

Jesus: It can be helpful, but it is not necessary. What is necessary is the truth between two hearts.

Paul: You seem to be willing to give people lots of freedom to explore who they are together, yet such freedoms have been infrequently offered by churches and temples. Why is that and why are such freedoms necessary?

Jesus: Most churches or temples want to maintain the status quo. They are interested primarily in their own survival and success. They want their flock to be like sheep. They are interested in control, not empowerment. I, on the other hand, am interested only in empowerment. I want to set people free to find their own truth.

When I walk past the cage, I always set the birds free. Birds that can't fly forget that they are birds. Humans who don't grow and explore forget that they are free to choose their own lives.

SEXUALITY

Paul: You are committed to freedom, yet you have a very conservative position on sexuality. What about sexual experimentation and the freedom to explore one's sexuality?

Jesus: I would not want to take away anyone's freedom to explore any aspect of their experience. But I want to be clear that engaging in sexual behavior of any kind without love for the partner is dispiriting. It is not uplifting for either party. But certainly I want people to be free to find this out for themselves.

Paul: What about sexual love? Is there such a thing as love that expresses only on the physical level?

Jesus: You are talking about physical attraction. That may be part of loving someone, or it may not be. Only you know when you really care about someone and when you are simply treating that person as the object of your own pleasure.

Paul: What if both people are giving each other pleasure. Isn't the mutuality the key?

Jesus: Yes, it means that the experience is valuable to both people.

Paul: Then why would you say sex without love is harmful?

Jesus: Because the act of having sex with a person opens the heart. It creates a certain intimacy. If that intimacy cannot express itself in the lives of the lovers then frustration and conflict will occur. Only if the heart is shut down can you be sexual in a casual way without experiencing frustration. And then the sex will be addictive and unsatisfying.

Paul: So it's not that sex without love is "evil." It's just that it creates suffering.

Jesus: That's right. If you want to avoid suffering, you don't engage in this behavior. But sometimes people have to find out for themselves that this is the case. You can't save them from the need to have their own experience.

RAPE

Paul: What about rape?

Jesus: Rape is a crime against the hearts of both people. It is the ultimate betrayal of the body at the hands of a mind that is convinced it cannot give or receive love.

Paul: Is that true for the victim as well?

Jesus: You can never say that anyone wants to be raped any more than you can say that anyone wants to be murdered. This is not an experience that we choose consciously. But that does not mean that there is nothing to learn from the experience. If you have experienced rape, you cannot heal without forgiving yourself and without forgiving the perpetrator. You can go on judging yourself or holding grievances against the other person, but you cannot heal. You cannot be free of what happened until you forgive.

Paul: So forgiveness is the lesson?

Jesus: Forgiveness is the lesson whenever anyone attacks you. First, you forgive yourself. You tell yourself "I am not bad or unworthy in any way, even though I have been attacked. It is not my fault. I do not deserve to be abused." You learn to stand up for yourself. Then, you forgive the other person. You say: "He didn't feel lovable either. He was expressing his self-hatred. If he loved himself, he could not possibly attack me. I can feel his pain, but I'm not responsible for it. He needs to take responsibility and learn to love himself. Then, he won't need to attack others."

With understanding and compassion, you release him. And in releasing him, you release yourself.

Paul: You can forgive the other person and yourself, but that doesn't mean that the other person will reciprocate.

Jesus: That's true. It just means that you have stopped carrying the burden of resentment or guilt. Others have to make their own choices. The point is that no one can hold you back once you have chosen to forgive.

LOVE IN THE MIDST OF FEAR

Paul: How do you walk the line between giving people the freedom to discover truth for themselves and preaching moral values which, if observed, will help them avoid suffering?

Jesus: You teach spiritual principles, but you encourage people to test out these principles in their daily lives. You want people to verify the truth in their own experience. If they accept the teaching without verifying it, they will imprison themselves in a dogma that prevents them from discovering who they really are.

Paul: Why is it so necessary for us to discover who we are?

Jesus: Because you have specific gifts you need to learn to trust and to share with others. You also have specific lessons to learn that will help you go beyond past fears and limitations. If you don't express your gifts and overcome your fears, what kind of life will you have lived?

Paul: It will be a failed life, will it not?

Jesus: Yes, in the sense that you have failed to live up to your potential. You have failed to do what you are ready to do. But that doesn't mean that you won't get another chance. There are no permanent failures. Even when you are afraid to be present, you can learn how to love yourself in the midst of that fear.

Paul: Isn't that the essence of what we are all doing here?

Jesus: Yes, learning to love yourself in the midst of your fear. That's all there is. When you can do that, you will hear Lao Tzu's belly laugh. Buddha will wink at you. I will shake your hand. From there to enlightenment is just half a step.

Paul: And what is that half step all about?

Jesus: Don't worry. You'll know when you get there! There's nothing I can say to you that will help you prepare for it. Just work on loving yourself when each of your fears comes up and enlightenment will happen by itself.

ENLIGHTENMENT

Paul: Is enlightenment a peak experience?

Jesus: Only in the sense that you feel at your peak when you are in the bottom of the valley!

Paul: You don't experience emotional lows any more?

Jesus: You experience them, but you don't give any energy to them. So they come and they go. When the wave comes and you are in the trough, you let it wash over you. Then, suddenly, the next wave lifts you up and you are flying. It's exciting.

You enjoy the ride, but you don't get attached to it. Surfing is a necessary life-skill, not a job description or a leisure activity.

Paul: So you don't seek out positive experiences or avoid negative experiences?

Jesus: That's right. You get out of the way and let Spirit take charge of life your life.

DWELLING IN THE PRESENT MOMENT

Paul: That sounds like a lot of the training I have been going through since you came into my life. You kept telling me to stay in the present moment and know that the words I needed would be given to me. You asked me not to take notes or to plan talks or workshops. I've learned to do that, but I sometimes wonder if a little bit of a plan isn't a good idea.

Jesus: Whatever comes to you spontaneously in the moment is what's important. That's where the energy is. Without that energy, you will be speaking words, but they won't mean anything. When I tell you to just show up and to be present, I am asking you to be totally open to what needs to happen. If you come in with an agenda, you can't be that open. Also, your agenda doesn't take into consideration the needs of the people who are coming to share with you.

Paul: But people always want to know what I am going to speak on and I can't tell them anything.

Jesus: You can tell them that you will speak on whatever God wants you to speak on and if they really want to know they'll have to come and find out. An evening with Paul Ferrini is an evening with Spirit. It is not a lecture on a specific subject.

Paul: Easy for you to say. You don't have to speak.

Jesus: You know perfectly well, I am with you whenever you open yourself to me!

Paul: Yes. I know that.

Jesus: I also think that you know that it works best when you can just be yourself in the silence. When you are ready to be present without any disguises, you are the manifestation of the Christ presence. That is more powerful than calling upon me to speak through you.

Paul: Yes. I sense this. When I can be present and when others can be present and authentic with me, it seems that we go deepest. We really touch into our lives in a powerful way.

Jesus: Yes. The key word here is "authentic."

You are not pretending to be what you are not. You are each just sharing in a trusting and respectful way from your own experience.

GETTING QUIET

Paul: People are very curious about what I do when I bring your words through. The only thing I can say is that I just get quiet and I hear the words. I don't leave and let you come in. You do not usurp my presence in any way. You simply amplify it.

59

Jesus: That is a good description of it.

Paul: A lot of it seems to be related to my willingness to remain in the silence.

Jesus: Well, the silence is the holy place: the tabernacle. When we go into the silence, we get ready to receive the word of God. The most profound understandings come when we can be quiet and listen to the voice within.

Paul: Would you say that getting quiet is one of the cornerstones of western spiritual practice?

Jesus: Yes. It is the foundation for everything else. It is like preparing the soil to receive the seed. If the soil is of poor quality, the seed will not stand a chance, no matter how strong it is. If you don't take time to set aside your neurotic, conflicting thoughts, you won't be able to hear the voice of God, even though you might really want to. When you can set aside your conflicting thoughts, reveries about past or future, and just be present, God can speak intimately to you.

Paul: Is it God who speaks to us or just our own higher consciousness?

Jesus: I know that this is an important question to you and to others, but the truth is there is no difference between the two. When you are in touch with your higher consciousness, you are in touch with God. Your higher consciousness has its being in God and it also lives in you. It is the link between your experience here and eternity.

Paul: And every person has that link, right?

Jesus: Yes everyone has it. But not everyone knows s/he has it. And even those who know it can't always be still long enough to experience it!

HOW TO ENTER THE SILENCE

Paul: What is the best way to get still?

Jesus: Deep breathing to bring the focus totally into the body. Then long, slow, measured breaths. No forcing. Let the mind follow the breath. If thoughts come, let them dissolve into the breath. Keep your awareness of the breath strong and it will be like a powerful river, sweeping along all that is dropped into it.

Paul: And how long should one be still in this way?

Jesus: For ten to twenty minutes. Longer times are okay, but don't think that you will necessarily have better experiences if you are quiet longer. Instead of going longer, it is better to have more frequent times of silence. If you could do ten minutes out of every waking hour, you would experience heaven on earth!

Paul: That's quite a statement.

Jesus: It's a true statement. Try it and see for yourself. When awareness is that strong a part of your life, you cannot act reactively. Every thought and feeling is given to the river, sooner or later.

Paul: And of course the river flows to the sea.

Jesus: Yes, the river flows to the sea. That is the final resting place. Once in the sea, the river has no more separate identity, nor do you or I.

CHANNELING 2

Paul: So the whole notion of channeling is a pile of spaghetti, because who is channeling whom?

Jesus: That's right. There is no barrier between you and I. Without a barrier between us our communion and communication are instantaneous. There is no need for a channel.

Paul: Channeling implies a separation that must be bridged by the channel?

Jesus: Yes, and, if there is no separation, who needs a bridge? The idea is ludicrous!

Paul: Well, there are a lot of people who think that if something isn't channeled, then it is just coming from the ego of a person.

Jesus: Well, the ego itself is a fiction!

Paul: I think that perhaps people are attempting to describe a non-dual phenomenon with dualistic language. Anyway, let's go on record here. Is there any such thing as channeling?

Jesus: No one channels anyone else. It would be like saying you are channeling Paul. Why would you say that when you could just be Paul. If you can be Jesus, why channel him?

Paul: Am I being Jesus?

Jesus: Yes, in a way you are. But even this description is misleading if you think that by being Jesus you cease to be Paul.

Paul: We are talking about a relationship, are we not?

Jesus: How can you talk of relationship when there is no separation? The word "relationship" itself implies that there are two separate entities who are "relating." This is not the truth. It may be what you perceive, but it is not the truth.

NON-SEPARATION

Paul: So when you say that whatever we do to someone else we are doing to ourselves, you are speaking literally? We perceive a separation that is not there?

Jesus: That's correct. Whatever you do is done to yourself. There is no other. There is no human being you can dismiss as separate from you. Even the murderer and the rapist. They are you and you are them.

Paul: And I am also Jesus and Buddha and so is the murderer and the rapist.

Jesus: Yes. Jesus and Buddha know this. But the murderer and the rapist do not.

Paul: So we are talking about states of consciousness or degrees of awareness. We are not talking about people in different bodies.

Jesus: People in different bodies simply physicalize different states of consciousness. One who kills or rapes believes in separation. He thinks he is different from you and he is afraid of you. He is defensive in his approach to you and to others. His body and mind are both armored. But the Buddha knows who you really are. Buddha knows who the rapist really is. You cannot fool Buddha.

A COURSE IN MIRACLES

Paul: Okay. Now I'd like to change the subject and get your ideas on what has been happening with *A Course in Miracles.* There is a great copyright battle going on now. Why was the *Course* copyrighted anyway?

Jesus: The intention was to retain the integrity of the material itself, but it has now gone far beyond that. Now it has become a attempt to control the use of the material, which is antithetical to the spirit of the Teaching.

Paul: I guess some people want to turn the *Course* into a Bible.

Jesus: Yes, that is what happens. First they make a Bible. Then they make a Church. Then they make a Pope.

Ironically, this material was presented as a self-study course. It wasn't meant to have an organization around it to protect it or regulate its use.

Paul: How do you feel about this?

Jesus: I am very excited about it actually!

Paul: You are excited about it?

Jesus: Yes, the *Course* establishment will act in such a rigid manner that people will be turned off and drop the whole thing. And that's what they need to do. Too many people have a parasitic relationship with this teaching. They cling to it as if it was the only truth. They hang on each sentence, each word. They quote chapter and verse, as if words were going to release them from suffering.

Those who need the words are only being held back by them. It's time to go beyond words and concepts.

The *Course* was a beacon to guide passing ships. Now it has turned into a busy harbor. There's so much traffic, boats cannot make it in and out any more. The whole thing has become narrow, one-dimensional. A teaching that was meant to bring intellectual liberation just created a new type of intellectual bondage. Helen got what she wanted, but now she can see the futility of it.

Paul: What exactly do you mean when you say that Helen got what she wanted?

Jesus: Helen wanted a course for intellectuals that would bring them closer to God.

Paul: Well the *Course* did do that for a lot of people.

Jesus: Yes. For those ships that came into its harbor, loaded up their cargo bays and left, it has been a tool of empowerment. It has opened up the next door. That door was different for each one. But the *Course* was a universal key. It opened a lot of different doors. The problem now is that everybody wants

65

to go through the same door. And there is no way they will all fit!

Paul: You mean that people are trying to make the *Course* be the door, instead of the key.

Jesus: Yes, that's right. The *Course* is a key given freely to each one. It will open the appropriate door at the appropriate time for that person. Each person must listen within and follow his own guidance. That is what the *Course* teaches. If one doesn't learn to listen within, then one doesn't have the key. One has an abstract belief system with no power to influence life. One stands impotent before the door, unable to open it.

Paul: To use the key you must say goodbye to the *Course?*

Jesus: Yes, sooner or later, the *Course* must cease being an authority. You must find that authority within. The *Course* can help you open the door to the temple within, but once that door is open, the key is no longer necessary. Throw it away or pass it along to someone else.

Paul: So the *Course* is a temporary tool that empowers, not an end in itself.

Jesus: That's right. And those who are fighting about the copyright think the *Course* is an end in itself. It has become their new authority.

Paul: So Helen knows that the path can never be strictly an intellectual one?

Jesus: Yes. Intellect can be the horse that leads you to water.

But it can't make you drink. A lot of the horses that come to the river are still staring at their reflections on the surface of the water. They are mesmerized and have forgotten that they are there to drink and then be on their way.

Paul: Pretty soon they will start charging admission for horses to stare into the water!

Jesus: That's okay with me. The further they take it, the better the chance that they will finally understand how absurd the whole thing is.

Paul: Are people addicted to the *Course?*

Jesus: Yes. That's why I asked you to start a 12 step program for recovering *Course in Miracle* students!

Paul: Right!

Jesus: Can you think of a better way to say it?

Paul: Not really.

THE AUTHORITY PROBLEM

Paul: Doesn't this relate to what the *Course* calls the authority problem?

Jesus: Yes. But it is actually two authority problems. The first one is that you should not be giving your power away to an outside authority like the president, the pope, the *Course*, or me. The second one is that you should not be giving authority to your own ego.

To put it simply: nobody knows any more than you do about what you need. And you don't need what your ego thinks you need.

Paul: How can we stop listening to the voice of our ego?

Jesus: Well, your ego's perceptions are practically married to the emotional and cultural expectations others have of you. And that is true even if you are reacting to those expectations.

To find out what you really need and who you really are, you must be in the silence for a long time, long enough for the ego-mind to stop buzzing.

Paul: Is that why it is so important to connect the mind with the breath when we go into the silence?

Jesus: Yes. When mind and breath are not connected, you see things through the curtain of your judgments and your reactive emotions. But when mind and breath are connected, the fabric of consciousness becomes more transparent.

LISTENING TO THE INNER VOICE

Paul: When the veil becomes more transparent, we begin to hear our guidance and follow it, right?

Jesus: Yes, you connect with the true authority within. This happens in the silence when the thinking mind stops buzzing. There is profound peace and gentleness in it. There is nothing impulsive, rash or reactive about it.

Paul: It's the still small voice within.

Jesus: Yes, but when you hear that voice clearly, it doesn't sound "small" at all. It's not like a mouse with a squeaky little voice, but like a lion roaring.

Paul: Are you saying that the inner voice is fierce?

Jesus: If you listen, the voice becomes a roar. That's what Abraham, Isaac and Moses experienced. It's what happened to Mohammed, St. Francis, the Baal Shem Tov and Rumi. It's what happened to me. And it is what will happen to you too, if you are willing to listen.

RELIGION AS RESOURCE, NOT AUTHORITY

Paul: If we are called to listen to the voice of truth within our hearts, why do we need religion?

Jesus: You do not need religion. At it's best, however, religion is an open book containing a record of other people's experiences. You can read in that book about my experience, or Confucius' experience or the experience of the ancient Vedic sages. It becomes a huge repository of knowledge that you can study. Study is not bad in itself, as long as it takes you back to your own experience. If it takes you away from your experience, it is not helpful.

Moreover, there are things that cannot be learned by reading scriptures or by talking to other people. There are things that are beyond words or concepts. You can experience these things if your mind and heart are open. You can't experience them if you are lost in your books or trying to live your life according to someone else's rules.

Paul: Isn't most religion dogmatic and prescriptive?

Jesus: Much of the commentary is. But if you go right to the horse's mouth after he drank from the stream, you can feel a cool sensation in your own throat. The lives of the masters are a symphonic poem with great emotional power and versatility. Why deny yourself the sharing of these experiences?

There is no reason why you need to turn the music off unless it creates a dependency in you. If hearing someone else make music prevents you from making your own, then turn the music off.

Paul: So understanding something about the spiritual experiences of others can be helpful if it doesn't take you out of your own experience.

Jesus: Yes. To some it will be enormously helpful. It will give them confidence. To others, it will be seductive and confusing.

Paul: How can you tell if it is helpful to you or not?

Jesus: If you need it to give you the answers, then it is not helpful. It will take you away from the process of finding your own answers. If you don't rely on it for answers, it can be a tool that helps you discover the truth within.

When religion is an open book that you consult freely from time to time, it is great! It's a library of experience. But if the doors slam shut as soon as you cross the threshold, you'd better realize it's not a library you've entered, but a prison.

Paul: Religion without the freedom to question and challenge authority is truly "the opiate of the people."

Jesus: Yes it is. People need to realize that religion can be a drug just like alcohol or heroin. In fact, sometimes the addiction to religious dogma can be harder to kick than the addiction to drugs and alcohol!

Both drugs and dogmatic ideas can be addictive. And people can go from one addiction to another, often giving up substance abuse for the new high of Bible-thumping, evangelical religion.

Paul: There are even a few *Course*-oriented communities that offer that kind of cult experience!

Jesus: The *Course* is not immune to any of the distortions that occur when human beings take charge of a teaching they don't fully understand and haven't fully internalized!

Paul: Yes, I know.

I like your metaphor of religion being like a library that one visits to get information. Nothing is forced on you. You don't have to join up, pay dues, or go out and convert the heathen. You just come and go as you please. I guess in an enlightened society, there would be no priests, rabbis, or ministers, just skilled librarians!

Jesus: That's right. You would tell them what you want to learn and they would guide you to the resources that could help you learn it.

Paul: Doesn't that lead to the secularization of religion though?

Jesus: Religion has already become completely secularized. Trying to speak to people in words they can understand isn't going to dilute their spiritual experience. If anything, it will enhance it!

71

Part Two

More Questions

RELATIONSHIP AND ALONENESS

Paul: I'm in a relationship that demands a lot from me and I haven't been able to take the time to write. Since writing is a major way that I commune with God, I have felt somewhat disconnected from my Source. I haven't figured out how to ask for alone time without my partner perceiving this as a way of disconnecting from her. Can you help me get some perspective?

Jesus: You must not be involved in a relationship that does not honor your work.

Paul: That's all you have to say?

Jesus: If your partner does not understand your need to write, then you are wasting your time in the relationship.

Paul: This seems very uncompromising.

Jesus: I find it interesting that you compromise on the issues that are most important to you, and yet on the less significant issues you refuse to compromise. I would suggest changing your priorities around!

Paul: I am trying to make changes. In the past I have not made my relationship my primary focus and, as a result, I have not given to the relationship what it needs.

Jesus: You cannot starve yourself and feed the relationship! Feed yourself and then the relationship can be fed.

Paul: My partner has come a long way to be with me. I am

her primary support. When I am not present for her, she wonders what she is doing here, and rightly so, I think.

Jesus: Then let her wonder. Sacrificing your writing will not serve her or yourself. Be honest with yourself and with her!

Paul: I don't honestly know. I see us doing this dance of drawing each other near and pushing each other away. It is a familiar dance, hardly one that is unique to this relationship.

Jesus: That dance may be familiar, but that does not mean that it is a good dance for either one of you to be doing.

Paul: I've never been in a relationship in which that dance did not occur.

Jesus: That is because you have never been so comfortable with yourself that you didn't care whether or not you were in a relationship.

Paul: Well, that may be true. I continue to have the perception that I am happier when I am in a relationship.

Jesus: Consider that for a while. Is it really true?

Paul: In some respects, it is true. In other respects it is not true. I enjoy the feelings of emotional comfort and closeness. But I miss the autonomy and the freedom of being alone.

Jesus: That is the truth.

Paul: Yes, that is the truth.

Jesus: So when you are in a relationship, you yearn for the

freedom of being by yourself, and when you are by yourself you yearn for emotional closeness of being with another person?

Paul: Yes, and I don't think I am alone in that.

Jesus: To be sure!

Paul: So where does this bring us?

Jesus: It brings you to a very simple question. Can you accept these swings of the pendulum when you are in relationship? Can you accept them when you are not in relationship?

Paul: You are asking me if I can dance with the ambivalence?

Jesus: I am asking you if you can be with one and allow yourself to want the other?

Paul: That's a good question. I keep wanting both and, if I am honest, I realize that the two are not particularly complementary. They are two very different orientations.

Jesus: That's right. Hence the conflict of being in one while wanting the other!

It helps to know if you are stronger standing alone or stronger standing in relationship. Standing where you are strongest will bring the most ease and fulfillment.

Paul: I have always felt that I was stronger standing alone, but I sometimes wonder if that is just the result of fearing intimacy. I wonder if I'm afraid to really be vulnerable and share my doubts and fears with another?

Jesus: It could be fear of intimacy, or it could be commitment to self.

Paul: Well, that's quite a swing. Is it heaven or hell?

Jesus: Either one could be hell.

Paul: How could commitment to Self be hell?

Jesus: It is hell if you are constantly trying to undermine that commitment by entering into relationships in which you compromise or betray yourself!

Paul: I guess that's true and I guess that it's also true if you keep entering into relationships without being able to open up fully to the other person.

Jesus: That's right. Being in a relationship in a frozen state isn't fulfilling, nor is being in a relationship because you think that you have to be. The truth is that you don't have to be in a relationship if you don't want to be or if being in a relationship is too scary for you.

Paul: But don't we have to face the fear of intimacy, if we have it?

Jesus: Well, I can assure you that you have it. I can also assure you that forcing yourself to face it when you are not ready is not a good idea. You can face your fears only when you are ready. Try to do it sooner and it will be a disaster.

Paul: Are you saying that some of us are not ready to be in relationship?

Jesus: Most of you are not ready to be in relationship, but that doesn't seem to stop you, does it?

Paul: I guess we get attached to being hit upside the head!

Jesus: I don't think you like it that much. In fact, every time you try to be with another person and it doesn't work, your self-esteem takes a substantial beating.

I think it is better to go into relationship slowly and cautiously. Intimacy is something that develops gradually as trust is established. Jumping into relationship is dangerous because, no matter how much you want the relationship to work, it isn't going to work unless and until trust develops.

Paul: So we put a lot of pressure on each other by trying to partner right away.

Jesus: Yes. You jump right into the frying pan. Is it any wonder you get fried?

As if that wasn't enough, you also beat yourself up mercilessly for jumping into the pan!

You are too anxious to mate, so you don't do it easily or gracefully.

Paul: We don't court long enough?

Jesus: It is not courting that prepares you. It is friendship and the gradual development of trust and respect for the other person.

Paul: Why do we rush things so?

Jesus: Perhaps it is because you think that there isn't enough time to let things evolve organically. Someone comes along who seems interested and you say: "If I don't act now, this opportunity may never come again." You don't trust yourself. You don't trust your own natural urge toward union.

Paul: How do we do that?

Jesus: You do that by being who you are and seeing what evolves without any pressure or any agenda.

Paul: You mean that you date?

Jesus: You spend time with people doing things that you both enjoy. Then, you see how you handle your differences when they come up. There are always differences between people in beliefs, temperament, values and interests. As you get to know each other, these differences surface. Then you see if you can respect the differences. You see if you can be together without agreeing or having the same experience.

This moment of truth happens in every relationship. If you have built a strong foundation, your house doesn't fall down when the first storm comes along. Differences arise, but you do not lose sight of what is shared.

No relationship succeeds that doesn't eventually carve out the space for each person to be alone. For example, you need to be alone to write. You can't take your partner into your office and have her sit down next to you at the keyboard. This is something that you need to do by yourself. If you don't do it, you will stop feeding yourself. And if you stop feeding yourself, your relationship is doomed.

Paul: Yes, I know that in my heart of hearts.

Jesus: You see, you must ask for what you need in the relationship. If she cannot honor your need to write, then she is not an appropriate partner for you. But please do not start thinking that she is an inappropriate partner for you before you ask for what you need and see how she responds.

Never try to anticipate what other people can or will do. Ask them in a heartfelt way and give them the opportunity to be honest with you.

Anyone who is threatened by your writing or your alone time would be far too big a burden in your life. It would not take very long before you were completely exhausted, and even then, all the concessions you made would not be enough.

When you aren't meeting someone's needs, it doesn't mean that you need to try harder. It means that you need to stop trying and just let things be. Then, you can face the truth and make whatever choice you need to make.

GIVING AND RECEIVING

Paul: Can you talk about the law of giving and receiving?

Jesus: Giving and receiving are two halves of the same coin. Without one, you cannot have the other.

Each one of you is a container for the love energy of creation. When you rest in acceptance, you become an open channel for that energy. When you resist or shut down, that energy cannot move through.

The real question is not "Is love there?" but "Am I open to receive love." Love is always there, but you are not always open to receive it. And if you cannot receive it, then you cannot give it either.

When you don't feel love inside your heart, you don't think you have anything to offer to others. It isn't true, but in such moments it would be hard to convince you otherwise.

Love is circular. What you put out touches others and comes back to you. What you hold in cannot reach others and so it cannot return to you.

Paul: So, in a way, loving is a very selfish act.

Jesus: I suppose you could say that. Loving others is good not just for them, but for you too. Of course, the contrary is also true: not loving others is harmful not just to them, but to you too.

Paul: So when we withhold love we only hurt ourselves?

Jesus: Absolutely. You may think you are punishing someone else. But you are really only punishing yourself. Others can decide to overlook your lack of love, but you hold yourself hostage to it. You are like a criminal robbing yourself at gun point.

Paul: That's an interesting image.

Jesus: Yes, you are stealing from yourself. By not giving love you are preventing yourself from receiving it. This is a form of self-abuse.

Paul: I can see billboards on buses and in subway trains that say: Love Others. It's good for your mental and physical health and well-being!

Jesus: Great idea! Why not have a marketing campaign for love? It can't possibly hurt anyone, and it will help hundreds of thousands of people in ways that you can't begin to imagine.

LOVE WITHOUT SACRIFICE

Paul: I have been away from this writing for a long time, a time in which I saw the relationship I was struggling with come to an end and a new, more fulfilling relationship evolve. In fact, it feels that my life partner has finally come into my life.

Jesus: And why do you think that?

Paul: Because she and I have a natural affection and respect for each other. It's not hard for me to care about her. In fact, it's effortless.

Jesus: That's one of the signs of spiritual union.

Giving to the other person is an act of pleasure, not sacrifice. One does not need to think about it. One just does it naturally. It is like a stream spilling into a chasm. It doesn't try to contain itself. It just lets itself go.

And receiving love from the other person is like drinking water when you are thirsty. You don't sit and wonder if it is wise to open your mouth. You reach for the glass without thinking.

Giving is a pleasure and receiving is a pleasure. Indeed, if you were asked to choose between the two, you would be unable to do so. They are so intricately related.

Paul: It seems to me that you stop thinking in terms of meeting your own individual needs when they conflict with the needs of the other person. You don't want to do anything that is going to be difficult for your partner. So you step back and see if there is a way that the needs of both people can be met or at least addressed.

Jesus: In other words you stop being self-obsessed!

Paul: Well, I didn't want to put it so bluntly.

Jesus: Why not? The truth is that most people care about meeting their own needs even if it means treading on someone else's toes. That's what the word "trespass" means.

You take what does not belong to you or—in a more veiled fashion—you appropriate for yourself what belongs to others as well as to you.

This breaks trust between people and undermines the entire social fabric. God warned Moses about that. If you look at the Ten Commandments, you'll see that this is one of the major themes addressed.

You can't even begin to talk about spirituality unless people trust each other. And trust does not develop unless people are aware of their trespasses and ask forgiveness for them.

That is why I asked you to pray "Forgive us our trespasses as we forgive those who trespass against us."

Paul: Sometimes it's hard for me to admit that I am wrong, but I do realize it and try to make up for it in other ways.

Jesus: I guess there's more than one way of asking for forgiveness. Some people can do so in words; others are more comfortable doing it in actions.

However, I encourage you to use words as well as actions. Saying "I was wrong and I'm sorry for what I did or said" is therapeutic for you and for the other person. It really helps to release feelings of guilt and resentment.

It also teaches humility, which isn't a bad thing for you to learn!

Paul: You're right.

FORGIVENESS: PART 2 OF THE TRILOGY

Paul: Asking for and offering forgiveness seems to be perhaps the most essential part of your teaching.

Jesus: Yes, it is. It is part two of the Judeo-Christian trilogy.

Paul: I'm not sure what you mean by that?

Jesus: Well, part one was the Ten Commandments. They told us what we should not do.

And the teachings of forgiveness are part two. They tell us what course of thought and action we must take when we have made a mistake.

Even though the Ten Commandments are fairly simple and straightforward, you'd be surprised how difficult it is for people to keep them. And what do we do with people who break the commandments: excommunicate them, put out their eyes, feed them to the lions?

A religion that preaches vengeance or punishment of sinners will eventually be overturned by the people. The "eye for an eye, tooth for a tooth" system of justice actually reinforces the trespass by repeating it. It is essentially hypocritical and people eventually see this.

If you truly believe "Thou shalt not kill," how can you kill the killer?

My teaching and the teaching of forgiveness in general proposes to address violence and trespass in a different manner. It suggests that we model the behavior we are expecting from the other person.

If the other person is fearful and strikes out at us and we respond in fear, we have validated his behavior by repeating it. But if we respond to his fear with love, we have stood for the truth and offered him an alternative.

This is not easy to do, but it is necessary.

We cannot teach truth by committing error. Only by acting in a truthful manner can we teach what truth is.

Paul: So, part two is learning how to forgive others. Isn't it also about learning to forgive ourselves?

Jesus: Absolutely. When you forgive the other person, you are saying "I have made the same mistake and so I forgive his" or you are saying "there but for the grace of God go I. If I did not feel loved I too might act in such a fearful way." You are identifying with this person and making him an equal. Forgiveness always happens between equals. That's why in forgiving another, you also forgive yourself.

You see, there are two stances you can take in the face of trespass. One is to say: "I did not trespass. You did. And therefore I am better than or stronger than or more spiritual than you." You can even use this argument to justify punishing the other person. But this means that you are holding everyone including yourself to the same standard of perfection. As soon as someone falters—and one day that someone might be you—there will be a price to be paid.

The other stance you can take says "While I did not trespass and you did, your trespass reminds me of my own fear and my own weakness. I know that one day I too may make the same mistake. I would be patient and have you learn from your mistake, knowing that one day I may need your patience to learn from my own mistakes."

This stance forgives the criminal and makes his redemption a central issue. The other stance condemns the criminal and makes his redemption a side issue of little, if any, importance.

Since you live in a world where commandments are broken, are you going to insist on perfection and punish those who are not perfect? Or are you going to acknowledge imperfection and help those who make mistakes to learn from their mistakes and come back into alignment with themselves and others?

Are you going to forgive trespasses or punish them? This question is no less topical today than it was two thousand years ago.

Paul: That's true.

REDEMPTION: PART 3 OF THE TRILOGY

Paul: So, if forgiveness is the second part, what is the third part of the trilogy?

Jesus: The third part, of course, is redemption. The trilogy is a simple one: sin, forgiveness, redemption.

If you look at it in terms of the soul's journey, part one represents the state of ignorance of Spiritual Law in which mistakes are made. Part two represents the state of knowledge or study in which we see our mistakes and become willing to learn from them. And part three represents the state of Atonement or Grace in which we begin to act in harmony with the laws of Spirit.

Paul: You aren't talking about a linear process here where we move from stage one to stage three and are then finished with the journey, are you?

Jesus: No, the journey is circular. You go through the three stages many times in reference to different lessons you are learning.

And it isn't at all unlikely that on certain issues you get stuck in a particular stage and don't move through as quickly as you are capable. But in these cases the pain of your resistance usually intensifies and you have a stronger incentive to learn what you need to learn.

PROJECTING OUR GUILT

Paul: I'd like to ask you about the phenomenon in which we take offense at the way someone has treated us. When things don't go our way, we often feel slighted or abused, and then attack back.

Yesterday, for example, a man who bought some tapes from us wrote that we weren't spiritual people and he was going to tell all of his friends not to have anything to do with us, all because we would not give him credit for tapes he had already opened and listened to.

Now, I can understand that he might have been disappointed by our policy. But it is a policy we apply to any person. We weren't singling this man out for special "unfair" treatment. Yet his response to us—his need to attack us and call us names—suggests that he felt that he was a victim of our abuse and had the right to retaliate.

Now, I understand that we are all capable of this kind of behavior. This man is not at all unique. What he did yesterday, I have done and seen many others do.

Jesus: I'm glad that you realize that this is a tendency you share.

The question you pose is a very important one. "Why do you feel personally attacked when you don't get your way. Why do you have such anger at God or at your brother?

I could tell you it is because in those moments you forget who you are and who the other person is, but this answer won't help you very much.

I think it might help you more to tell you that you act on a false assumption. You assume a attack, when no attack may be intended.

Paul: I know this was a big problem for me in my previous relationship. After weathering a few attacks, I assumed an attack was coming and became defensive even when there was no threat present. The perception of "attack" triggered me.

Jesus: Yes, that is what it is: "a perception." If you don't perceive an attack, no attack happens.

Paul: That's a very powerful statement.

Jesus: Yes, it is. It is what I demonstrated on the cross.

Paul: Please say a little more about this.

Jesus: Men were pounding nails into me and I felt excruciating pain. But I never perceived attack. I never blamed the men who were doing this to me. I knew that they were acting out of ignorance and had cut themselves off from the source of love and compassion inside themselves.

If they had understood and felt the suffering they were causing they would have immediately stopped these actions.

Paul: Won't they have to feel this pain some day?

Jesus: Yes, it is very likely that they will have to feel it to understand that it is a wrong behavior. And so, yes, I had compassion for them even as they were hurting my physical body, because I knew that they might have to experience this kind of pain too.

Paul: As we give, so do we receive.

Jesus: Yes, this is the law. It helps us become aware of the consequences of all of our actions.

TAKING OFFENSE, GIVING OFFENSE

Paul: So why do we feel attacked sometimes even when no attack is intended?

Jesus: You assume that other people want to hurt you. They may be acting out of their own fear and frustration, yet you assume they have singled you out.

Of course, many times people do try to make you responsible for their own anger and frustration. They come at you saying "it's your fault" and, if you react to them fearfully, you will be buying into their delusion.

But, if you don't buy into it, if you say to yourself and to them. "It's no one's fault . . . not yours or mine" you can step outside the circle of blame.

That means that you know that you are innocent and so are the other people. By not being a target, you recall them to their innocence.

They attack you only because they identify with the accusations they are making of you. What they see in you is what they are afraid of in themselves. That is their hidden or unconscious guilt, which they are afraid to look at. So they try to give it to you. They accuse you of the crimes they have committed or are afraid they are going to commit.

By hurting you, they externalize their own guilt or fear so they can look at it.

Paul: But they don't look at it, do they?

Jesus: No, not usually. They try to hide it by giving it to you. But if you overlook their attack and offer forgiveness, you don't accept that gift. Instead, you say "Sorry, this guilt does not belong to me. To whom does it belong? You offer them the opportunity to claim it and release the pain and sadness behind it. And if they do, you tell them "It's all right. It's not so terrible. I am willing to forgive you. Can you forgive yourself?"

You help them acknowledge their guilt and offer forgiveness to themselves. It is an extraordinary process.

Paul: What if we take offense when no offense is intended? Does that mean that we have our own guilt to face?

Jesus: That's right. Why otherwise would you take offense?

Paul: So we never take offense where we have not given it?

Jesus: Absolutely. I see you are getting good at understanding this.

Paul: Well, I have a good teacher.

So, getting back to the original example, the man with the tapes takes offense because he has treated people the way he assumes we are treating him. He feels guilty about it, but his guilt is unconscious, so he tries to give the guilt to us. Then, he feels justified blaming us for his own error and thus continues to avoid awareness of it.

Jesus: Interesting circle of delusion, is it not?

Paul: I guess that it all comes back to fact that we don't want to acknowledge our own mistakes and, if we don't acknowledge them, we can't learn from them.

Jesus: That's right. You stay stuck in the Ignorance/Sin stage of unconsciousness. You never make it through to the stages of Understanding and Atonement.

Paul: And that's the karmic circle, is it not?

Jesus: Yes. That's it. You don't get off the wheel of fear until you begin to face your own fears and take responsibility for them.

Paul: No wonder we make so little progress here.

Jesus: In spiritual terms, that is correct. Some individuals are able to move through their karmic dramas, but most are not. That's why the collective consciousness continues to be fairly unconscious, projecting its hidden guilt on a vast scale. Is it any wonder that mutual trespass and vengeance continue between members of different economic groups, races, religions, or countries? The more you try to hide the dark side, the more volatile its expression becomes.

THE NEXT DIMENSION?

Paul: I recently went to a Conference in which many people, including a few who say they talk with you, maintain that humanity and planet earth are poised to make this quantum leap into the next dimension. I don't see this, do you?

Jesus: Many people have a great deal of trouble being here right now and taking responsibility for their thoughts and feelings. You don't get to the Atonement dimension unless you do the middle step and raise your fears into conscious awareness.

Paul: So you don't see this major transformation happening on the planet?

Jesus: Transformation is an internal affair, not an external one. When people have faced their fears and stopped projecting them, the world will be at peace. People will care for each other and for the planet. That will be the natural result of the inner transformation happening in people's hearts and minds.

Paul: Is there some kind of celestial speed up going on?

Jesus: The only speed up going on is the one happening on earth, driven by rampant consumerism and constant technological innovations.

From the celestial perspective, what's happening on earth is just a tiny drop in a very big bucket. Of course, that doesn't mean that what is happening here is insignificant. It is very significant for you.

IN, BUT NOT OF THE WORLD

Paul: Is it possible to live in a way where we don't get drawn into our own dramas or the dramas of others?

Jesus: Yes, but obviously it takes a certain discipline. This is what I meant when I said you needed to be "in the world" but not "of the world."

"In the world" means that you participate in life fully. "Not of the world" means that you don't need to try to change anything external to find your peace, because you know that your peace is within. Peace is found in the heart, not in the world.

Your peace does not depend on what happens to you. It depends on who you are.

You can work for the things you believe in, but don't be attached to any particular outcome. If your side wins, be grateful, but don't celebrate at the expense of the other side. If your side loses, be sad, but remember that you are more important than what you believe in and so are the people on the other side.

Having things your way does not make you happy. If it does, then your happiness is a precarious thing.

Paul: Can you say a little more about this?

Jesus: We all think that we will be happy as soon as we get XYZ. XYZ can be a job, a relationship, money, prestige, you name it. But then XYZ comes and we find that we aren't happy.

That's because happiness is an unconditional state of consciousness. It isn't dependent on having something else.

If you are a happy person, not having a job, not having money, not having a relationship and so forth doesn't depress you. On the other hand, if you are an unhappy person you can have all of these things and be wounded and depressed.

Paul: We seem to want what we don't have.

Jesus: Well, you see, wanting and not having are the same thing. If you have, you don't want anything.

If you are happy, you don't strive to be happy.

If you have just eaten a huge meal, you aren't hungry. You don't need to go around looking for food.

Paul: Are you saying that dinner is available, we just don't want to eat it?

Jesus: Yes. What you need is right before your eyes. If you find fault with what you have, it can never suffice. You cannot find beauty in it. You cannot be happy or satisfied.

ORDERING FROM THE MENU

Paul: I guess there is a big gap between what we want or think we want and what we need.

Jesus: Yes, there is. For example, if you need protein and I give you a fish, it will certainly meet your needs. But if you don't like fish, it won't be what you want. What you need and what you want aren't always the same.

Paul: We don't always like the menu life offers us, do we?

Jesus: Certainly not always. And, even when you do, that's no guarantee that the food will be cooked to your liking or served to you in a manner that pleases you.

Paul: So our wants are the cause of our suffering?

Jesus: It's not that you shouldn't want what you want, but you need to realize that you aren't always going to get it. One time, fish is the only thing on the menu. Another time, you order chicken, but it arrives burnt. Are you going to be upset or will you be gracious?

When the joke is on you, are you going to laugh, or take out your gun and shoot the waiter?

Paul: That's a rather interesting choice.

Jesus: Sometimes you just need to understand that "today is not a day when I am going to get what I want." So when dinner is burnt and your car won't start and you miss an important meeting, and the drunk on the street laughs at you, maybe you should be laughing too. Some days, no matter how good you are and how hard you work, you aren't going to get what you want.

Are you going to take it personally? Are you going to make it be someone else's fault? Or are you going to realize that the stars are just a bit crossed today and it isn't a reflection on you or on anyone else.

Paul: Yes, you are right. Some people die of rare diseases and it's not because they are bad people.

Jesus: No, they are not bad people any more than you are a bad person because you got burnt chicken on your plate. You have to deal with your life the way it is. Just because you want it to be different doesn't mean that it will be.

Paul: Is there some sort of blessing in suffering?

Jesus: There is a blessing in acceptance and dealing with life with a positive attitude, even when it is not easy. There is a blessing in submitting to the lessons of life. But I wouldn't say there was a blessing in suffering, unless by suffering you mean "allowing" life to take its course.

Paul: Is this what Job did?

Jesus: Yes. Job allowed life to reveal itself. He stayed with it even when it was extremely unpleasant. He could have blamed God and turned away from Him. He could have blamed others for his problems. But he did not. He submitted to life and, in the process, his faith was greatly tested. His story is your story too. On one level or another, life rarely shows up the way you want it to, and then the question is "How do you hold it?"

Paul: You mean "do we shoot the waiter?"

Jesus: Yes. Or do you realize that the waiter is just doing his job and it's not his fault any more than it is yours?

Paul: Well, what about the cook? Isn't it his fault that the chicken is burnt?

Jesus: Well, go into the kitchen and ask to speak to the cook then. There aren't many cooks who will answer you. Most will point to someone else and say: "It's his fault, not mine. He had the flame too high." The best that going into the kitchen can do is produce a scapegoat. It's not worth the time and energy it takes to establish someone else's guilt. So why bother?

Better to let it not be a crime. Better to laugh, forgive, feed the burnt meat to the dog. Fortunately, he can't tell that the chicken is burnt and just gobbles it right up.

Now how guilty can that cook be if he just fed your dog?

Paul: You sure have a knack of putting the best face on the situation.

Jesus: Well, I'll show you two faces. One is angry, distraught, vengeful. The other is jolly, peaceful, loving. Which one do you want?

98

Paul (jokingly): I'll take the angry one!

Jesus: Very funny.

Paul: Well, you make it all sound so simple and even easy. But it isn't easy.

Jesus: When you perceive the situation in a true light, it is easy to choose peace. The hard part is perceiving it correctly.

TRUTH IS TRANSFORMATIONAL

Paul: Do you have any suggestions about how we can perceive things more accurately?

Jesus: First, you need to see what you want or expect the situation to be. See your own investment in it. Then, just let it be what it is.

Don't beat yourself up for wanting it to be different. Just see what you expect and then let it be as it is.

Paul: So you accept the situation and you accept that you have expectations that were not met?

Jesus: Yes. You accept the outer situation—however it appears to be. And you accept the inner situation—whatever disappointment, resistance, or frustration you feel.

Paul: You look objectively without and honestly within.

Jesus: Yes, that honesty is essential. You see that you wanted things different and they are not different.

Paul: What is transformational about that?

Jesus: Truth is always transformational. Sometimes when you are honest with yourself, the external situation changes. Sometimes the external situation stays the same, but there is an internal shift enabling you to perceive it differently.

Paul: So the primary goal is honesty: seeing the situation the way it is?

Jesus: Honesty is the beginning. First you see it the way it is and then you open to any deeper truths that may be present.

For example, someone has an auto accident. First, he must come to grips with what happened to him. He needs medical treatment, massage, physical therapy. Then, as he is taking care of himself, he sees that this accident has enabled him to slow down and get more connected to himself. By accepting and working with the situation the way it is, he tunes into its inner meaning. He realizes that he must not go back to the old stressful lifestyle he had before.

Paul: Is there always such an inner meaning behind every event or circumstance in our lives?

Jesus: Yes, the inner meaning is always there, but that doesn't mean that you are ready to acknowledge it.

Opening to the truth about yourself and your experience is a process. The more willing you are to learn, the more your experience opens to you.

INTEGRATING THE INTELLECT

Paul: Soon, we will be celebrating your birthday. How has your mission to us changed in the 2,000 years since you lived on this planet?

Jesus: The biggest change has been the development of the rational intellect and the need for approaches to spirituality that respect and integrate the fruits of scientific inquiry.

I do not expect you to believe on faith or to live an unexamined life. I encourage you to investigate and find out the truth both in your world and in your heart. Open minded questioning and observation are not in any way opposed to spiritual development. Indeed, they enhance it.

The danger of your time—and you have all experienced it many times over—is the tendency to take the rational intellect and make it an infallible God. Then, you lose touch with your intuitive mind, which is just as important as the rational mind. Emotional realities that add tone and richness to human experience are disrespected. And your approach to religion becomes one-dimensional. It loses touch with the mystery.

Paul: We begin to think we know everything.

Jesus: Right! Knowing is important. But knowing what you don't know is equally important.

When you live in the unknown, you can often penetrate far deeper into the nature of truth than you can when you think you know what something means.

To put it simply, mystery is not bad. Not knowing is not a weakness. What is harmful is thinking that you know when you don't. Prejudice, narrow-mindedness, hubris, pride—these are weaknesses.

Paul: It's interesting to me that you consider the development of the rational intellect to be a positive thing, considering its capacity to dominate our experience in unhealthy ways.

Jesus: Well, once again, it is a matter of balance. It's not good for one part of the mind to dominate the other.

When the more emotional aspects of mind dominated, you had ignorance, magic, superstition, inquisitions and holy wars: not exactly the most edifying or compassionate manifestations of human consciousness!

Paul: I guess passion and dispassion have their upsides and downsides. Would you say that we are moving toward an integration of these two sides of mind.

Jesus: Yes. You are moving from heart vs. mind to heartmind.

Clearly one of the challenges of your time is to move toward syntheses of many of the polarities of the past such as male vs. female, black vs. white, Christian vs. Jew, science vs. religion.

You are looking to find the higher perspective, the commonalties between opposing views, the unity within diversity. It is a very challenging time and a very good time for the refinement of human consciousness.

Paul: So you are not completely pessimistic about this time on planet earth.

Jesus: Not at all. You are struggling with many of the same lessons that human beings have always struggled with. In that sense, there is nothing new under the sun. On the other hand, you are breaking free of many of the intellectual rigidities of the past and, in that sense, a new age is being born.

Paul: But this is not the age that we call "New Age" is it?

Jesus: Well, it is in the sense that it suggests popular access to information once available only to a few. Yet the internet probably underscores the possibilities of the New Age more than books on esotericism or yoga.

One aspect of the new age is that it brings things to light. It requires that knowledge be available to people who need it, not hidden away in rare books or secret societies.

It also means that that which has previously been seen as dark and shameful must come to light. Hence, you have a famous actor on trial for cutting his wife's throat and a president on trial for having sex with a young girl. And you have people whom the state has put to death proven to be innocent.

All the unseemly aspects of your collective humanness must be seen for what they are. Pretense must be dropped in favor of honesty with oneself and others.

Paul: But this greater visibility of both our knowledge and our ignorance does not guarantee a better world.

Jesus: No. It is just the first step. Once you are aware of an inequality, a misperception, or an injustice, you can acknowledge it and say "this is false." Once you are aware that something is true, you can affirm that truth and live in harmony with it.

Paul: So we see the beginning of the New Age with the opening up of what has been dark, hidden or obscure, but we don't see the end of it. We don't know if it leads to greater freedom or greater bondage. We don't know if it will result in a "new renaissance" or a "brave new world."

Jesus: No, the jury is still out. Indeed, you are the jury. You are the ones who will decide.

BUILDING A REAL DEMOCRACY

Paul: What do you make of the Supreme Court's ruling in effect choosing the next president of the U.S?

Jesus: This deadlock in Florida was very important because it showed all the problems with the election process. Clearly, this was not the first time such problems have existed, but because of the closeness of the election it was the first time these problems were scrutinized. What was dark and hidden about democracy in the U.S. is now out in the open, and the system can be revised so that is fair to everyone.

Moreover, if an election can be decided by 500 votes, it means that everyone's vote counts. You can no longer say "it doesn't matter whether I vote or not." The act of voting goes from being an inconsequential act for an alienated and/or disenfranchised minority to being their essential duty to themselves and their country.

Paul: Of course, many people do not vote because they feel

that they have no choice. They don't see many significant differences between the two major candidates.

Jesus: Obviously, for democracy to work you need candidates who reflect the full spectrum of peoples' ideas and values. That means candidates must come from the rank and file, not just from the higher echelons of money, power and privilege.

Paul: Well now we have a former wrestler as the Governor of Minnesota!

Jesus: You see, give the people a chance and they will show you a little poetic justice!

Many people with great wisdom and leadership ability are not considered as candidates for public office because they are not professional politicians and/or because they don't have sufficient money, power or privilege. Indeed, I doubt that an Abraham Lincoln could get the nomination of either party right now. Maybe that's something you should think about. America isn't coming close to tapping the depth of its leadership potential.

Paul: Not only that, but it's time we had a plumber, an electrician, or . . . maybe even a carpenter for president, don't you think?

Jesus: Sure. I know a lot of good carpenters!

DARKNESS & THE COMING OF LIGHT

Paul: It is just two days to the winter solstice, the time when there is the least daylight and the most darkness. Can you comment on this symbolic time and indicate why it is connected with the time of your birth?

Jesus: Darkness and light are not only physical phenomena; they are metaphors for consciousness. That which is illumined can be fully seen, while that which is dark is hidden or shrouded in mystery. Light symbolizes knowing, dark unknowing.

All cycles have a low point and a high point. The low point represents both the end and the beginning, the alpha and the omega.

Midnight is the low point in the daily cycle. New Moon is the low point in the monthly cycle. And winter solstice is the low point in the yearly cycle. These three low points represent times when the old is ending and the new is being born. It is a rather inward, contemplative time when you evaluate the successes and failures of the past and anticipate the promises and challenges of the future.

It is not a time of activity, planning or preparation. It is not a time that supports action or ambition, but a time that supports rest and introspection.

It seems to me completely clear why I was born into the world at such a time. It was time for a new teaching, a new understanding, a new relationship between people and their God. The old way must have run its course and people were thirsting for a new gospel. I came in answer to the prayer of their hearts.

Paul: Is that also why you were born in humble circumstances: in a manger, to a man of simple means, a carpenter, and a woman of simple faith?

Jesus: Yes, my birth was inconspicuous, except to a few wise men who anticipated it. They knew the time was ripe. They were astrologers. They knew the old age was ending and the new one was beginning. They knew the planet was ready for a "world teaching," a teaching that would not exclude anyone, but was meant for all.

John (the Baptist) knew it best. He felt it deeply in his heart and he saw it in my eyes when we met. And so he was the one who first acknowledged me and announced my ministry.

Paul: So you came at the darkest hour?

Jesus: Yes, I came at the time of the Caesars when the Roman state was in its greatest dominance. Secular power was pervasive. The Jews could not challenge this power, so they adapted to it. It was the low point of Judaism. The fire of the faith had almost died out. It had become a few smoldering embers.

I came to fan the flames, to set hearts on fire once again, to offer people an alternative to the trivialization of the faith. My birth was the sign that the Roman Empire had past its peak and had begun to decline. It was simultaneously a sign of the beginning of a spiritual rebirth.

The power of the kings was about to be challenged. For me, God alone could be king and, in my ministry, even God would cease to act like a king. He would no longer keep distant from His creation but, through me, He would reach out and care for them.

It was also a time when all human beings were ready to be challenged to recognize their equality. No one was to be higher or lower than another. I required that my followers accept their brotherhood and interdependence.

Paul: Well, I'm afraid to say that your teaching seems to have fallen a bit short of the mark! We still have a few kings around, although maybe not as many as there were 2,000 years ago. And people are still struggling with the issue of equality.

Jesus: Yes, I know. But I came to show the way, not to take the journey for you!

WHO IS THE CHRIST?

Paul: Isn't it true that you are the Christ?

Jesus: Yes, but so are you and so isn't everyone else who learns to love and accept self and others.

Paul: But this is not something most of us believe.

Jesus: If you don't believe you are the Christ, try walking in the way of Christ. Practice what I came to teach you and you will begin to realize that the Christ nature is the essence of each person.

If you see it in me, you must also see it in yourself and in your brother or sister. If you don't, it is not Christ that you see, but some form of specialness valued by the world. True equality cannot be experienced by human beings until they acknowledge that the Christ lives in each one of them.

Paul: Are you saying the Christ is some sort of collective phenomenon?

Jesus: Yes, Christ is the light born in the darkness. It is the flame of self acceptance that extends to others and eventually to all. It is the flame that becomes a burning bush and in time a bonfire.

Christ comes at the time of greatest darkness, the time when inner power is ignored and outer power dominates. He is rebirth of love in a world driven by fear.

The fact that I accept my Christhood is significant because if I can do it so can you. Now that you know this is a potential for you, you will not stop until you realize it, no matter how long it takes.

Your assignment is clear. The time that you take to accomplish it is unknown, even to you.

Paul: So are you the Messiah or are we still waiting for him/her?

Jesus: Whenever any person wakes up, the Messiah is born. Your freedom cannot be contingent on what someone else does or does not do.

The Messiah's job is not to do your homework for you, but to be a model of that state of consciousness that occurs when the homework is done.

Paul: Are we waiting for everyone on the planet to wake up?

Jesus: I hope that you aren't waiting for others to wake up when you can wake up right now. Why wait?

Waiting doesn't help others. Waking up does help, because then there are more models around for people to see.

Paul: Is there some sort of magical number of people who need to wake up for the earth to become a place of peace?

Jesus: One in a hundred is a good possibility. One in ten is better.

Paul: When you say wake up, what exactly do you mean?

Jesus: I mean that you become completely open to love. You become a way in which love can express itself, a channel through which love is given and received.

Paul: Obviously, this does not happen overnight.

Jesus: Not usually. Usually, it is a process in which you see the truth and start living it, embodying it, expressing it, however imperfectly, in your thoughts, words and deeds.

Paul: So each day gives us numerous opportunities to open to love.

Jesus: Yes. The question is are you aware of those opportunities and are you taking advantage of them? And if not, why not?

Paul: That's a good question for us to ponder during this solstice and this Christmas season!

Jesus: Yes, it is a good question to ponder each day when you wake up in the morning. Each day is a new beginning.

MESSIAH: THE INNER CHRIST

Paul: I want to continue talking about this idea of Messiah. Are you saying there is no Messiah?

Jesus: I am saying two things which appear to be contradictory, but really aren't.

First, Christ is the potential of every human being. I am not special. So in this sense, there is no Christ who stands apart from you. Moreover, there very much is a Christ who stands with you. You have but to acknowledge him. Call this the Inner Christ, if you will.

The Outer Christ—be it Jesus or Buddha or Krishna— comes and goes. But the Inner Christ is always with you.

The Outer Christ is simply one who knows the truth and teaches it. That is what I did. The Outer Christ calls out to the Inner Christ in you and empowers that One to come forward.

Paul: But this is so different from the orthodox Christian teachings that envision you as the Messiah, the only Son of God who died for our sins and through whom alone we can receive salvation!

Jesus: I understand that, but consider that proposition closely and you will see it is nonsensical.

If your salvation depended on me, then there would be nothing you could do to bring it about. All your good deeds, all your loving thoughts would be for naught.

That would overturn the very foundation of the Jewish teaching. And I can assure you that I did not come with that mission. Mine was a mission of re-awakening the truth, not of changing it.

111

I taught that without surrender to God the moral teaching was meaningless. It could not bring an insincere person into alignment with the Divine Will. Actions alone were not enough. The intention behind the actions had to be pure.

I taught that it is not just the law but the spirit of the law that matters. But I never said "throw out the law."

Obviously, not stealing, not lying and not killing are necessary for living a spiritual life. There is no question that these commandments need to be kept. Anyone who says it's okay to lie, cheat, steal or kill is teaching untruth.

But it is not enough just "to refrain" from negative behaviors. We must also embrace positive behaviors. That means sharing what we have with others, telling the truth, and even risking our own lives to help others.

My gospel was not a "thou shall not" gospel, but a gospel that asked specific things from you: to love, to forgive, to be fair, to share your life, your wisdom and your resources with others.

I simply restated the moral agenda. I told you what you needed to do with your whole heart to come into alignment with the Christ within. Coming into that alignment is your salvation, because it brings you to the authentic truth about you and about others.

I am not your salvation. Your salvation lies in your surrender to the Christ within. But I am your model. I am a witness for the truth standing before you, reminding you. And those who accept my teachings and practice them are also models. This is how the teaching extends to others.

Then, through your own practice and the support of a loving community, these teachings are internalized. When that happens, you don't have to quote chapter and verse. You don't have to say "Jesus said this" or "Moses said this." You don't need to wave your Bible in front of people.

When the teaching is internalized, you become the teaching. You hear the words of truth spoken in your heart and they are given to you whenever you need to speak them to others.

Paul: So how we act toward one another does matter?

Jesus: Yes, your actions do matter. Morality is an important aspect of spirituality. A spiritual person does not just speak the truth, but also demonstrates it through his or her actions.

Paul: But are you not also saying that spirituality depends on something greater than us?

Jesus: I am saying that spirituality depends on something greater than your ego consciousness. But that "something" is not outside of you. It is in your heart of hearts. That something is the Inner Christ.

The Inner Christ may not be visible to you. It may be hidden in some inconspicuous place—in some manger where beasts of burden lie—but sooner or later you will be led there and you will pick that child up and celebrate him. That will be the true Christmas, because that will be the day that you accepted the Christ Within.

Paul: Christ comes at the darkest hour.

Jesus: Yes, Christ comes when you have the courage to look with love at the most fearful and shameful aspects of yourself.

Paul: So seeing with compassion does not mean that we refuse to see our own suffering or that of others?

Jesus: No. You must see what is there. But you must also see it through the eyes of truth. You know that the light is there, even in the deepest darkness. And you are not afraid to call upon the light.

When you call upon the light, you acknowledge and affirm it. It comes at your call because it belongs to you.

It does not matter if you have denied it or rejected it in the past. It remains there awaiting your call.

Paul: No wonder you don't claim to be our savior.

Jesus: If you left the lap of God, you did so of your own free will. And you must return there the same way.

Others can point the way, but you must take the journey.

THE BODY OF CHRIST

Paul: So you are a way-shower, not a savior?

Jesus: Yes, I am a savior of myself and therefore a way-shower for you.

Paul: What does it mean when you save yourself?

Jesus: You return to love without conditions. You understand that all conditions you place on love create suffering for yourself and others and so you cease imposing these conditions.

You love because that is your nature. It doesn't matter if that love is returned by the person you offer it to. Her response does not matter. Because you offer love to her, you also offer it to yourself and to all beings. No one stands outside your love or apart from it.

Paul: You are talking about complete unselfishness.

Jesus: Yes, in the sense that you care for the good of others as you care for your own good. But you do not stop caring for your own good. You never stop loving yourself, no matter how unpleasant people are to you. And because of that, you don't have to stop loving them.

Paul: Is this really possible?

Jesus: I am the witness that this not only is possible but it can happen for you. And I am not the only witness.

Paul: It is an extraordinary possibility.

Jesus: It is the promise of Christ that you may not only surrender to God's Will, but through that surrender become an expression of that Will.

This is the body of Christ. It is the Will of God at work in the world.

The body of Christ does not mean my physical body but the body that carries the message. All of the messengers live in the body of Christ.

Paul: And they don't necessarily belong to the Catholic Church, do they?

Jesus: The body of Christ has nothing to do with any church. It is the group of people who have internalized the teaching and have become is arms, its legs, and its voicebox. You, for example, are one of them.

Paul: I know that ever since you came into my life I have considered myself a mouthpiece for your teaching.

Jesus: Yes. It is my teaching, but also yours. It is my truth, but also your truth. It goes beyond the identity of anyone.

Indeed, it goes beyond the body. That's why it is somewhat ironic to call it the "body of Christ," unless you understand this to mean that Christ is working through many bodies.

Bodies are temporary and temporal. Christ is not.

When the Christ within awakens, you have already moved beyond the limitation of the body you inhabit. Indeed, you realize that this body is simply a device enabling you to do the job you have agreed to do.

FEAR OF DEATH

Paul: Then why am I afraid to die?

Jesus: You are afraid of losing the body because you have identified with it. You know you are not limited to the body, but you are still attached to it. You don't know how you will operate without it.

Will you still be Paul? Will you be conscious? Will you think and feel? Or will you stop being Paul, stop being conscious, stop thinking and feeling?

Paul: Yes, that's true.

Jesus: If I told you that you would still be Paul would it make you feel better?

Paul: Yes, except for the skeptic in me that might not believe you.

Jesus: Then you will have to wait and find out for sure.

Paul: I'm sure that others would like this question addressed.

Jesus: It is a difficult question to address. I guess you could call it a kind of "Catch 22." As long as you are attached to your body and afraid of losing it, you cannot have a certainty about your non-physical existence. Yet once you cease to be attached to the body, you have that certainty, so you don't have to ask the question.

Anyway, the answer to the question is not just a factual one. You know at all levels of your being, not just in your mind.

This kind of "knowing" is an aspect of faith, a way of trusting that which can never be completely revealed to you until it is experienced.

Paul: Are you saying the fear of death will remain until we die?

Jesus: The fear of death is also the fear of the unknown. The more you learn to trust the unknown, the easier it will be for you to open to death without fear. But do not be hard on yourself. Fear is your companion in life. Why would it be different in death?

THROUGH A GLASS DARKLY

Paul: You have made it clear that, although we can learn from others, yourself included, ultimately our salvation is our own responsibility.

Jesus: Yes. That's right. You created the drama of your guilt and so you must save yourself from it. It is a rather silly drama.

Paul: Why is that?

Jesus: Because not a single one of you is guilty per say. You simply don't understand that you are loveable and acceptable the way you are. So you attack others. And then you feel guilty for doing so.

The more unloved you feel, the more you attack. And, of course, others respond in kind. So you begin to feel quite justified striking back at them.

It doesn't take long before the cycle of violence is established and, with each turn, the mutual guilt proliferates. How can you feel innocent when you have hurt so many people?

You substitute a false reality for a true one and you believe in that false reality and make it real every day with your fearful thoughts and actions. Your brothers and sisters do the same. The world you live in is a world of your collective creation. You are all certain of its existence, but its reality is essentially false.

When the false assumption you made in constructing this reality is challenged, the world you made will be disarmed and the cloak of sorrow removed from it. It will be a different world than the one you perceived before, a world freed from the darkness through which you perceived it.

This is what he meant when our brother Paul said "first you see through a glass darkly, and then face to face." As long as you believe you don't deserve to be accepted and loved you cannot see your brother the way he really is. You see him through the dark lens of your fear and he sees you through the same distorted lens.

Paul: How can we see the world the way it really is?

Jesus: You must start by learning to see yourself the way you really are.

Stop for a moment and bring your awareness into your heart. Do you feel the presence of love there? Do you feel your love for others and their love for you? Is there a warmth and a glow there or a black hole?

If you love and accept yourself, you will feel that warmth, that inner radiance. If you don't, you will feel an emptiness and a yearning for that which seems to be missing.

I have told you many times that God's love for you flows through your love and acceptance of yourself. If you don't feel that love and acceptance, then that is where your spiritual journey must start.

You must stop looking for love outside of yourself and learn to give this love to yourself each day, each hour, each moment. This is intense spiritual work, but it will bring you immediate results, because it immediately challenges and overturns your false view of yourself.

By loving yourself, you begin to feel the presence of love. That makes it easier for you to reach out to others and easier for them to reach out to you. Instead of being a black hole, you become a tiny flame extending the light.

Paul: You are talking about tuning in to how you feel about yourself on a regular basis.

Jesus: Yes, I gave you the mantra. Simply ask yourself "Am I loving and accepting myself right now?"

And if the answer is "yes," please congratulate yourself. And if the answer is "no," please remind yourself that it is time to begin your spiritual practice.

Ask yourself this question at least three times per day when you begin this practice. Then, increase to once per hour.

When you get to this level of practice, it will become automatic. Then, when you are disturbed or lose your peace, you will hear your inner voice asking you "Are you loving and accepting yourself right now?"

And you will wonder "How is it that the question does not come from my conscious effort?" And you will realize that you have internalized the mantra, so it will constantly work for you.

Now, you are in communion with the deeper aspect of yourself, the awakening Christ Self. When this inner teacher takes over, you no longer need an outer teacher or an outer practice.

Now, every moment is practice. Life and spiritual practice become one.

Paul: So this is your method for spiritual awakening?

Jesus: Yes, this is the primary method. In addition, I suggest taking at least ten to fifteen minutes in silence at least twice per day to ask the question fully on all levels of being.

I also suggest practicing forgiveness of yourself and others on an ongoing basis.

This means that every time you judge yourself or another person, you become conscious of it and you forgive yourself for making that judgment. It also means that any time others judge themselves or judge you, you forgive them for making that judgment.

I have also offered you the Affinity Group Process* as a way of practicing forgiveness and building Spiritual Community on a weekly basis. This process synthesizes the original practice of confession with the Sabbath ritual. It is also very powerful.

If you do these practices in a heartfelt way, you will begin to surrender your fear and guilt and awaken your Inner Christ nature. But, mind you, I am offering you a lifetime practice that will lead steadily to peace, not a glamorous peak experience that you can brag about or put on your resume.

If you hear bells and whistles, great. If not, great. It makes absolutely no difference.

Paul: That reminds me of my friend Sean who always used to say "You hear a voice, but I don't hear anything. I don't see pictures. No matter how much I meditate, nothing happens." And he is one of the most spiritual people I know.

Jesus: Well, as you know, spirituality is not a fireworks show.

Paul: It's chop wood, carry water, clean the bathroom, etc.

Jesus: That's right. There's nothing special about it. It doesn't offer worldly rewards. If it did, it wouldn't be spiritual practice.

---

*Please see the book *Living in the Heart: The Affinity Process and the Path of Unconditional Love and Acceptance* by Paul Ferrini.

Paul: I guess there are a lot of religious organizations raking in millions of dollars and paying their leaders handsome salaries that might have some explaining to do then!

Jesus: Well, greed doesn't need much explanation!

Paul: I was going to be a little more charitable.

Jesus: Why be?
I told you "By their fruit, you will know them." If they use their wealth for the benefit of the poor and the sick, then they are fulfilling a spiritual mission. If they don't, their mission is the same as the companies that trade on Wall Street.

Paul: Well, my brother lives on Wall Street. But it's a different Wall Street.

Jesus: I'm glad for you and for him.

CAPITALISM AND ITS CHALLENGES

Paul: You aren't against capitalism, are you?

Jesus: Capitalism is very creative. In that sense, I like it. But it is not necessarily responsible for its creations. In that sense, I am not too happy with it.
I would like to see a creative economy that is responsible for what it creates and its effects on people and the environment.

Paul: Well, government tries to insure a certain degree of responsibility.

Jesus: Yes. And if that government is really responsible for meeting the needs of the people, then that is very helpful. But there is a better way.

Paul: And what is that?

Jesus: It's called self regulation. Right action. Do unto others as you would have them do unto you.

Paul: That is the moral imperative but, as you have pointed out, not all religious organizations are concerned with moral imperatives.

Jesus: Well, in the end, it comes down to the choice each person makes, does it not? You can't legislate morality, nor can you scare people into being good or responsible. Religion has tried to do that and failed across the board.

All you can do is decide for yourself and set an example for others. Individuals in business, politics, government and religious organizations can be models of caring and compassion. They can lead and inspire. I'm afraid that is the best that can be done.

Paul: Well, Communism failed to compel equality and Capitalism has a very long way to go to give birth to it. I guess we need to find a way to synthesize what's good for the individual with what is good for the masses.

Jesus: That is true. But really there is no difference between the two.

Paul: What do you mean?

Jesus: What is truly good for the individual is not at odds

with what is good for the social group. It is only when the individual acts in a selfish manner—which is not ultimately good for him or her—that group harmony is compromised. And, unfortunately, if you try to restrain individual expression because you do not agree with the ideas being expressed, you have the beginning of a police state.

Paul: It seems that we have to tolerate a good deal of diversity if we want to guarantee the freedom of the individual.

Jesus: Yes. At times you may have to put up with ideas and behavior that you find unwholesome, offensive, even obscene.

Paul: But isn't there a point at which that behavior becomes hurtful to others? For example, adults may want to buy pornography but, when children are exposed to it, it becomes harmful.

Jesus: Yes, but you cannot shelter children from every influence you disapprove of. At some point you need to realize that some exposure is inevitable and prepare your children for this.

Often, opposing something just makes it stronger. So you have to be careful. Regulation is an art form that few have mastered. Sometimes you need to say "No" absolutely. Sometimes you need to say "Yes, but only under these circumstances." Knowing when to take a stand and when to step back and allow is a skill only the greatest leaders have. They can be firm and remain compassionate. They can compromise and be vigilant at the same time.

Paul: I guess we always come back to the individual.

Jesus: That's right. That's where responsibility starts and ends.

Society can be only as responsible and as compassionate as its individual members. Leaders can influence, guide and inspire, but when they try to force people to be a certain way, they inevitably fail.

SETTING OTHERS FREE

Paul: Yesterday and today I have been feeling a lot of sadness because my son has decided to quit school and I feel that he is acting in a self-destructive manner. He's just begun to feel comfortable in school and to prove to himself that he can do the work.

Jesus: What is the nature of your sadness?

Paul: I feel that he is making a bad decision. He wants me to support it, but I can't.

Jesus: Can you love him and not support this decision?

Paul: That is the difficult thing. Of course, I still love him, but I am disappointed because I think he is deceiving himself. He thinks that if he just avoids responsibility, it will just go away and leave him alone.

Jesus: And you know that it won't.

Paul: Yes.

Jesus: Indeed you know that he is responsible for everything that he thinks, says and does, in every moment?

Paul: Yes.

Jesus: So you know that regardless of what he does he will have to face himself?

Paul: Yes.

Jesus: So why are you sad?

Paul: I'm afraid he just keeps going around in circles. Whenever something is a little hard for him, he tries to bail out. But he does not see it as bailing out. He sees it as a way of reinventing himself. Only he doesn't reinvent himself. After a few days all his grandiose ideas fall flat and he is left to pick up the pieces of his irresponsible behavior.

Jesus: So if this is his pattern, what can you do? Even though he is your son, you cannot force him to get off the treadmill. Let him stay on it until he gets tired. Then, he will get off of his own accord.

Paul: I'm afraid that he won't get off. He is standing on the edge of a black hole of depression. If he doesn't put any energy out in a positive direction, he will crawl into that hole and live in it.

Jesus: But you know very well he must be free to do what he wants to do.

Paul: Even if it will cause him pain?

Jesus: Yes, regrettably, even if it will cause him pain. You must let him make his own mistakes and learn from them.

Paul: Do I need to support him financially?

Jesus: That is up to you. If financial support keeps him from taking responsibility for himself, then probably not. But if it helps him to feel accepted and valued, then some form of financial support might be helpful. But it can be tied to his actions in supporting himself.

Paul: I think he might perceive that as a way of controlling him?

Jesus: Perhaps, but then he will do without your support in order to be free to make his own choices. And that might not be such a bad thing.

Paul: So I can simply say what I'm willing to do and leave it up to him.

Jesus: Yes, offer him what you can financially. Support him emotionally. Tell him you care about him and wish him the very best.

Paul: That's all?

Jesus: Yes, unless you want to hold onto your sadness!

Paul: No, I don't like feeling sad and powerless.

Jesus: So don't take responsibility that does not belong to you and drop your expectations of him. Offer him respect by allowing him to live his own life, even if you disagree with the way he is going about it.

Paul: It seems that you are saying "Let him go."

Jesus: Yes, let him go and let him come, as he wants to and needs to.

When he needs to leave, step out of his way. When he needs to return, receive him with love.

Paul: Isn't this a lot to expect of a parent?

Jesus: Perhaps, but it is what will bring you peace. Why not face the challenge squarely?

Paul: Perhaps you are right.

Jesus: The greatest challenge for any parent is to love the child and let him go. The fact that the child wants to go indicates his desire to have his own experiences and to learn from them. It is a positive thing. Sometimes, of course, the child may get in over his head and need to ask for help. But that is what you want him to do. You want him to feel comfortable asking for help. You don't want him to feel that he must do it on his own at any cost.

For example, this whole situation was precipitated by his getting lost while doing an errand for you. He called and asked for help, did he not?

Paul: Yes.

Jesus: And did you help him?

Paul: No.

Jesus: Why not?

Paul: Because he called me collect and interrupted me during an interview. He didn't have 35 cents to make a phone call to the store to ask for directions and I had just given him $90. I felt exasperated with him.

Jesus: Don't you see that he was telling you that he needed your help.

Paul: I do now, but at the time all I could see is that he was being irresponsible and turning a simple task until an unbelievably complicated one.

Jesus: So the question is are you going to allow him to be irresponsible and still love him and respond to him when he needs your help, or is his irresponsible behavior going to prevent you from helping him?

Paul: That's a good question. When he acts irresponsibly, I don't want to help him.

Jesus: Okay. It's good that you are being honest. But I want you to understand that it is precisely when he is being irresponsible that he most needs your help. Can you see that now?

Paul: Yes.

Jesus: So he is asking for your love and acceptance when it is most difficult for you to give it, right?

Paul: That's right.

Jesus: That is your challenge. That is your spiritual work in this situation. You need to move past your own disappointment with his irresponsible behavior to understand that he needs your acceptance and your help.

Paul: He needs to know that he can screw up and that it is okay?

Jesus. Yes. He needs to know that he can make a mistake—even a stupid one—and it will be okay. You will still love him. Right now, when he makes a mistake, he thinks that he's useless and he must do something to punish himself. So he acts in a self-destructive manner. He drops out of school.

Paul: Yes, he takes a small mistake and makes it into a huge one. He misses a couple of classes and is afraid to face his teacher so he just stops going to school.

Jesus: Because he believes that if he takes responsibility he will be crucified! He needs to learn that taking responsibility is helpful to him. It gives him an opportunity to become wiser and more skillful.

Paul: I'd love to be able to help him learn that.

Jesus: If you understand his pattern and don't play into it, you can reach out to him when he needs you. That will help both of you. Why not try it and see what happens?

Paul: Okay. It sounds right to me.

PARENTING THE PRODIGAL SON

Jesus: I'd just like to make one more point here. As a parent, your love for your child must grow. It begins as a kind of protective embrace that provides a sense of security for the child. And gradually it is challenged to open up and allow the child more and more freedom. With that freedom comes lots of mistakes, because that is how the child learns. And she can't learn to be on her own if Mommy or Daddy is always holding her hand.

Moving away from Mommy or Daddy is always a bit of a risk and it can be scary both for parent and child. But this is a necessary phase in the development of both parties. Parents need to learn to let go of inappropriate responsibility for their children and children need to learn to take appropriate responsibility for themselves.

Our relationship with God is much the same, except that here we are the child growing up and asking for more and more responsibility. God, being a wise parent, gives us the freedom to make our own mistakes and learn from them. Sure, He would like to jump in when we get in trouble and fix everything for us. But He knows that we would not learning anything if He did this.

So He has to stand back and watch while we make all kinds of mistakes and then crucify ourselves and each other mercilessly for the mistakes that we make. Indeed, sometimes He wonders if we will ever wake up and begin to take responsibility for our lives.

You feel exasperated with your son, but consider how exasperated God is with His Son! Indeed, it's a wonder that he can watch the absolute terror and absurdity of our dramas without intervening.

Now I realize that the Old Testament God may have intervened. But that is not the God that I know. He did not intervene when I suffered on the cross, nor did he intervene at Auschwitz or Hiroshima.

He is not going to do our work for us. When we reached the stage in our evolution when we wanted the freedom to know ourselves, God stepped back and allowed us to go through the door.

To be sure, many of us wish that we never decided to leave that place of safety where we knew that we were completely accepted and loved. But now that we have left, we can be sure that God is not going to rescue us. He is not going to jump in and save us.

But we can be sure that when we feel overwhelmed by our independence and reach out to ask for His help, He will not withhold it. He will be there when we call out to Him, because no parent ever abandons a child.

Next time your son calls on the phone, you will answer it and see how you can help him, even though you think he is involved in the most absurd drama. And, in the same manner, God will answer your call for help, even when you are suffering from your own brand of delusion.

God will not condemn you for making a mistake and you must not condemn your son. For you are a parent now, but you were once a child, who needed to be loved and accepted regardless of your drama.

If the parent cannot look beyond the drama, then he cannot be a parent. And if he cannot be a parent, how can he know that his son is innocent, and so is he?

FREEDOM AND RESPONSIBILITY

Paul: I'm still struggling with what's happening with my son. I keep thinking he will come to his senses, but so far he hasn't.

Jesus: What he senses and what you sense are two different things, are they not?

Paul: Yes.

Jesus: He wants freedom and you want him to be responsible. You know that there is no freedom without responsibility and he knows that there is no real responsibility without freedom.
You both have a valid point.

Paul: What do you mean?

Jesus: Well, you already understand that if he refuses to take responsibility it will limit his options. Therefore, he will not have true freedom to choose, because he won't be choosing from a full deck.

Paul: Right!

Jesus: But you need to understand that if the options that are available to him now are all repugnant to him, then he can't make any kind of meaningful choice, never mind be responsible for that choice.

Paul: That's probably true.

Jesus: So let him come up with his own options. Then, his choices will have some meaning to him.

Paul: In other words, give him enough rope to hang himself?

Jesus: Yes, except the rope isn't for hanging himself. It's for hitching up his horse. If he chooses to hang himself with it, there isn't much that you can do.
If you don't give him the rope, he will find another way to get it. And he will resent you for withholding it.

Give him the freedom he wants and he will learn responsibility. It is inevitable.

Paul: Is it that simple?

Jesus: Most of what you struggle with is very simple. You just resist it. That's what makes it difficult.

Stop resisting. Let it happen. Let him do what he wants to do.

Paul: I'll try.

Jesus: Trying isn't required. Just do it. Drop your expectations. Holding onto these expectations will just keep your pain going. There's no point to it. The hook is fastened under your shirt, not under his. Undo it, and throw it away.

Then he will be able to come and go when he pleases. Now, he avoids you because he doesn't want to get hooked. When he sees that the hook is gone, he won't have to resist you anymore.

If you give him his freedom, you free yourself too.

Paul: It always works both ways, doesn't it?

Jesus: Absolutely. What you give to others, you also give to yourself.

THE GIFT

Paul: I guess we often think we are punishing someone by withholding our love or acting in a hostile manner when in reality we are only punishing ourselves.

Jesus: That's right. So think twice before you give a slight, an insult or a curse, because whatever you give returns to you in one form or another.

Give as you wish to receive. Give love, emotional support, money, blessings, etc. Give with gratitude and receive what others give to you graciously.

The circle of giving is powerful. Respect it.

Consider what you have to give. Does it make you happy to give it? If not, do not offer it. For it will not be a gift of your heart. It will not be a true gift. What you give begrudgingly or out of sacrifice will not benefit you or others.

Ask yourself: "Do I value this gift? Is it something I am grateful for? Does it give me pleasure to offer this gift? Do I think it will benefit the person to whom I offer it?"

If the answer is yes to all of these questions, then you offer a blessing. If the answer is no, then please reconsider. Don't attempt to give what you don't value or want to hold onto.

Paul: Why is our own "valuing" of the gift important?

Jesus: Because it indicates that you are offering something that you think is important. Therefore, you can offer it enthusiastically and the recipient can feel that.

Paul: But what if the gift is not something we value, but something that we know the other person values?

Jesus: They can feel that too. The best gift is valued by both people. Then the benefits of the gift are immediately shared by both people.

Paul: But my benefit may be to see the smile on your face

when you receive this gift, even if it's not something that interests me.

Jesus: Indeed! That is a mutual benefit.

Paul: Mutuality seems to be an important concept to you.

Jesus: Yes. If something is good for one person, but not for another, there is some form of trespass or exploitation involved. And all who trespass must eventually step back. Any unfair advantage one person gains over another is temporary and temporal. Today's master is tomorrow's slave. . . . Better not go there.

When something is good for both people, there is no debt that needs to be paid, no wrong that needs to be righted. A lot of unnecessary suffering is avoided.

EVOLUTION AND DEVOLUTION

Paul: Are you saying that some kind of karmic debt is established when one acts in a way that is good for self but not good for someone else?

Jesus: Well, acting in a selfish way takes you into a lower orbit, so to speak. And, in that orbit, the people around you are likely to respond to you the way you respond to them.

On the other hand, when you act in a way that brings mutual good, you move into a higher pattern of alignment.

Paul: Could you expand on this a little?

Jesus: On the highest level of alignment, the good of the individual and the good of the group are one and the same. No one would consider an action that would be harmful to anyone else. Therefore, the integrity of the group pattern can be maintained.

Paul: So what we call sin or error is a tearing of the fabric?

Jesus: Yes. That is a good way of putting it. Selfish actions are divisive. They split things apart. They compromise or undermine the harmony of the whole.

Paul: Is this inevitable?

Jesus: Not at all.

If one person acts in a way that is divisive and everyone else reacts to it in a hostile way, then yes the integrity of the whole can be undermined. This is a kind of "devolution" in which the whole is split into its component parts.

But if people in a group do not react in a hostile way to the antisocial actions of one of its members, then the group can remain cohesive. Later, that member may be reunified with the group or his place might be taken by a more willing participant.

Paul: So evolution is a process in which we build higher social units based on the cooperation of people with mutual needs and aspirations?

Jesus: Yes. It is a joining. As soon as you accept that someone else's happiness is as important as your own, you have a new socio-spiritual unit. That is what marriage and family are all about.

Paul: Then how do you explain the prevalence of divorce in our world and the consequent break up of family life?

Jesus: When a form gets old, it needs to be re-created so that it speaks to the needs of the time. When old definitions of marriage no longer speak to people's hearts, they are rejected and new definitions are explored. The same is true for parenting.

People in your society are seeking a higher degree of freedom in their relationships. But more freedom means more responsibility and that is something you haven't come to terms with yet.

For example, if you are going to give your child the freedom to explore aspects of life you were never able to explore as a child, then you will need to increase the amount of time you spend supervising these explorations. Exploration without supervision means a lack of parenting.

In the same manner, if you and your spouse are both going to work in demanding jobs, often traveling separately to other states or countries, you are going to have to work much harder to make the time you spend together nurturing and productive. Otherwise, you are going to grow apart.

Freedom without responsibility is divisive. It allows expansion of consciousness, but it doesn't allow for the integration of the new material. Integration requires the feminine energy of discipline, structure, routine. It enables us to return to the center. Every home must have a hearth. The further you stray from the hearth, the harder you have to work to maintain it.

MALE AND FEMALE ROLES

Paul: Today, it is not uncommon to see men tending to the hearth while women work as the primary breadwinners. What do you think about that?

Jesus: Well, if both people accept this reversal of roles, there's nothing wrong with it. The woman can do the plumbing and the man can do the sewing. Why not? But when there's no plumbing happening, neither one can use the toilet. And when there's no sewing happening, both have to wear clothes with holes and buttons missing.

When neither woman nor man attends to the hearth, the relationship will have no safe harbor. Then, some kind of shipwreck is inevitable.

Paul: What about parenting roles?

Jesus: Well, usually the father sets the boundaries and encourages the risk-taking and creative ventures of the child, and the mother provides the nurturing and emotional support. But it could be the other way around. However, parents should not delude themselves. The child needs both the male and female polarities in place, regardless of which parent is providing them.

Paul: Isn't it easier for women to embody the nurturing energy and for men to model the creative energy?

Jesus: Yes, as a general rule, it is easier. But there are exceptions. And neither women nor men are as far apart in these polarities as they used to be.

Paul: So isn't it easier to accept and work with some flexible version of traditional roles, then to try to work away from them?

Jesus: Yes, it is always easier to swim with the current than against it. But there must be room for people to choose to swim upstream if that is what they want.

Paul: So let's get back to the idea of evolution we were discussing before. Whether people gravitate toward traditional or non-traditional values and roles, they are still challenged to put the good of their partners and children alongside their own. That is what is required for social and spiritual growth, is it not?

Jesus: Yes. And as people grow spiritually, their circle of loving and giving expands outward till it embraces other families in their community and, ultimately, the entire human family.

We are here to keep offering our gift of our love and acceptance until there is no one who stands outside the circle of our love, not even our enemy.

That is how peace comes to our hearts and to our world.

MINDING ONE'S BUSINESS

Paul: I am afraid that I haven't been very good about writing lately. I have been building a website and focusing on what I need to do to sell books.

Jesus: I know those aren't your favorite activities, but they are part of the ebb and flow of being in the world. No one gets to do exactly what he wants to do all of the time.

Paul: No one?

Jesus: Yes, no one. Life isn't a perpetual vacation. Sometimes it's hard work.

You might have a glorious vision, but then you must execute it. You might have a mental picture of a house on a stream with light streaming through the windows. You might even see yourself walking on the deck overlooking the stream, feeling the sunlight and listening to the sounds of the water moving below. But creating that house in the woods takes a lot of focused work. You need to find the land and prepare it. You need to design the house and build it. And along the way there will be many frustrating moments when you need to be flexible and adapt to the conditions at hand.

Paul: So in the middle of creating paradise we might be feeling irked or even downright angry because something isn't happening the way we want it to?

Jesus: Yes, you might be. Being in the world is not just about light. . . . It's also about the shadows that are cast when objects appear in the light. Light may be the ultimate truth, but that does not mean that you won't experience the shadow.

You can't escape the warp and woof of existence. That means that one moment you feel happy and the next moment you feel sad. No matter how spiritual you are or think you are, you can't experience only the highs and avoid the lows.

True spiritual growth enables you to experience the highs without getting puffed up and the lows without getting deflated.

Paul: You are talking about balance, are you not?

Jesus: Well, balance is the result of accepting all of our experience. If we accept both the highs and the lows, we end up somewhere in the middle, but it is not a place of compromise or mediocrity. It is a dynamic place created by a synergy of polarities. It is peaceful in the midst of chaos, or creative in the midst of routine.

Paul: In the east, they say it is "neither this nor that."

Jesus: Yes, that is one way of saying it. The other way is: "It is both this and that simultaneously."

Paul: Most of us think we get gray when we mix white and black, and gray seems a bit drab and unappealing.

Jesus: Well, sometimes gray is more white than black and sometimes it is more black than white. It is dynamic. It is always changing. Both black and white have the potential to explode into color.

Paul: How does this metaphor translate into our daily lives?

Jesus: If you are alert, the most marvelous opportunities for creative breakthrough exist in the daily routine of existence. You might think routine is boring, but it is not boring. It is black moving fiercely toward white and exploding into some heretofore unimagined color.

Paul: So even though I don't like attending to my business, there are possibilities for wonderful things to happen when I'm doing it?

Jesus: Yes, building as you know can be boring or creative. It depends on the attitude you bring to it.

The creative part is not just in the design phase, but in other phases as well. Selling books doesn't have to be any less creative than writing them!

Everything you do is important. Some things are not more creative or spiritual than other things. Creativity and spirituality come from the attitude of heart and mind we bring to the task at hand.

Paul: So I can learn to enjoy the business side?

Jesus: If you don't enjoy it, you will carry it like a cross and it won't prosper. Yours is a simple choice: either enjoy it or stop doing it.

Paul: Thanks for the advice!

Jesus: Why would you want to keep doing something you don't enjoy?

Paul: Because it pays the bills and I do enjoy the creative part. Besides, you started this conversation by saying we couldn't enjoy everything.

Jesus: Yes, that's true. But that's not because there isn't the possibility for enjoyment there. The possibility is always there.

But usually the reason you don't enjoy something is that you are not bringing to it the attitude of heart and mind that are required to enjoy it.

Paul: But it seems that you were suggesting before that we drop the expectation that life show up the way we want it to so that we can deal with the inevitable frustrations and problems that happen.

Jesus: Yes. That would be a wise thing to do. Don't expect life to show up the way you expect it to. Accept what does happen as gracefully as you can. Yes. This is all very good, but I am saying more than this.

Paul: Okay.

Jesus: I am saying that when something happens that you think is a problem, the "problem" might be in your consciousness, not "out there" in the world.

Paul: So first I should drop my expectations and accept what is and then I should look at the contents of my consciousness to see if I am creating suffering?

Jesus: Precisely.

THE POWER OF OUR BELIEFS

Paul: The subject of creativity and responsibility is a tough one. For example, some people believe that they give themselves cancer because their consciousness isn't "spiritual" enough.

Jesus: That is because they are confused between the inner and outer worlds.

Paul: Say a little more about this.

Jesus: We choose to bring a certain attitude toward "what is." And our attitude can be changed. Changing our attitude from a negative one to a positive one might make us feel a lot better. But that doesn't mean that if we feel better we won't have cancer.

We don't and cannot control everything that happens to us. We can determine to some extent how we feel about what happens. And that may have an influence on what happens in the future. But there are no guarantees that we will get the result we want.

That's why we always have to come back to acceptance practice: accepting "what is" and bringing a positive and creative attitude to it. This is the core of spiritual practice. And it does bring results, but not necessarily the ones we hope for.

Paul: So where does our responsibility lie?

Jesus: What you think and feel about something and what you do about it are your responsibility. Nobody else is responsible for what you think, feel or do.

Paul: So coming back to business: I'm responsible for what I think, feel and do about my business. I can determine how I feel about my business but not necessarily what happens in my business. Right?

Jesus: Yes. And if you want to feel good about it you need to accept what happens and think, feel and act in a positive way.

Paul: A very simple formula!

Jesus: All of my teachings are simple to understand. But they are not necessarily easy to practice.

The important thing is to understand that you have a dialog with your experience. That dialog can be either negative or positive. You can be negative and reactive and find problems everywhere. Or you can be positive and creative and see new opportunities.

The best business people do the latter. They might not be the "richest" business people, but they are the happiest.

Paul: I'd settle for "happiest."

A REVOLUTIONARY ACT

Paul: It seems to me that, while almost anyone can be creative, very few people actually are. Few people have a vision of what they want and even fewer still have enough confidence in themselves to bring that vision into reality.

Jesus: Most people are comfortable with what they know and fearful of the unknown. Creative, visionary people, on the other hand, can't wait to move into unknown territory. They aren't afraid of it. Or, if they are afraid, they don't let their fear hold them back.

Paul: Well, most of us want what other people want. We think that is what will make us happy. We never stop and ask the question "What do I really want?

Jesus: It's a dangerous question to ask! Because asking it forces you to understand and accept what it is unique about you. It is a revolutionary concept to consider that you can be true to yourself.

Paul: Yes. I don't think the Democrats or the Republicans, the Christians or the Jews, would like us to cultivate that level of independence.

Jesus: Right. Any group would have a hard time with it. Asking "who am I and what is best for me?" is not a group question. It is an individual question. And it is not an outer question. It is an inner question.

It does not have anything to do with the way things are. It has to do with the way you are.

Paul: Most people don't know who they are because they don't ask that question.

Jesus: That's right. The individual who asks that question does not accept the structure of authority nor the façade of normalcy that surrounds him and endeavors to control him. He or she rejects the norms of the group along with all its rules and "isms."

Paul: Yes, I understand. To become who we are authentically is a powerful act.

Jesus: Not only that. It is a spiritual imperative. You must know who you are. Or perhaps more importantly you must know who you are not. You must let outside definitions and expectations of you drop. You must become naked. That is, you must become the "essence" of who you are, with nothing added on.

When you have become completely and wholly you, nothing stands between you and God. You are like Adam in the Garden. You are an original manifestation, "created in God's image." You are one ray of the divine light.

Paul: Why does society try so hard to discourage us from this inward journey toward our true selves?

Jesus: Because human beings want what is predictable and familiar. They prefer to live inside the circle of their fears. They are afraid to cross over the lines they have drawn around their own experience. Were it not for the few creative, confident individuals who dare to step over these lines, social institutions would not grow. They would become increasingly rigid and disembodied. In the end, they would collapse from within.

EDUCATIONAL INSTITUTIONS

Paul: When you talk about institutions collapsing from within I can't help but think of the educational system in the U.S.

Jesus: Yes. There is great energy there waiting to be liberated, energy that cannot possibly be contained by the walls of the classroom. The effort to build new, stronger walls will only dam this energy up and create greater violence than what you see now.

The walls will have to come down. The energy will have to be liberated and guided into new channels.

Those who are used to building the walls of square rooms cannot build the schools of the future, which will have walls to climb, not to imprison.

Paul: So you see that this whole system will collapse?

Jesus: Yes, but that doesn't mean that people won't try to shore up the walls and hold them in place. Nevertheless, it will be a waste of time, energy and money.

The teachers of the future must begin teaching outside of the walls of the prison. Then, when the prison collapses, there will be places for people to learn about themselves and others. That, after all, is the real curriculum. And it cannot be legislated. It is an act of love and communion.

Paul: Speaking of communion . . . .

Jesus: Yes, I know what you are going to ask me!

The situation is no different in your churches and temples than it is in your schools. Passive people allow others to dictate to them. Creative people do not. Creative people ask difficult questions, even if they cannot answer them.

Those who wish to squelch or control the search for answers build the walls of their institutions very thick and put bars on their windows. And any institution—a school, a church, a business, or a government agency—can be a prison.

Large institutions are by their very nature difficult to move in new directions. Large governments, large corporations, large churches, etc. want to preserve the status quo.

How can you expect them to empower the individual to find himself? They are the engines of conformity, not creativity.

ENGINES OF CREATIVITY

Jesus: Small, decentralized groups of people joining together to support the asking of the "big" as well as the "small" questions about life are the breeding ground for original ideas.

Without the strength of small entrepreneurial ventures, capitalism would be no more successful than communism has been.

Paul: So capitalism survives because it creates a climate in which individuals can innovate?

Jesus: Yes, but every coin has two sides. The individual must be free to create something he believes in, but if he does not create something that people want, he won't survive in business.

The problem is that, even in a capitalist society, the individual is so quickly socialized that his or her chances for genuine individuation are small if not actually rare. The educational system almost guarantees the perpetuation of the status quo.

Of course, I am not saying that there should be no norms.

Certain behavioral norms are essential for maintaining safety. But when too many rules are made, you start to rebuild the prison of mediocrity.

Does everyone have to wear uniforms? Does every student have to learn French or Geometry?

Let us not forget that Moses came back from Mt. Sinai with only ten Commandments, not with thirty five. Unfortunately, my Jewish brothers and sisters decided that ten commandments were not enough. So they took ten simple guidelines and turned them into 613 rules regulating nearly every aspect of life.

If God wanted people to "behave" that badly, he would have created robots, not human beings. By all means, let us have behavioral norms that support safety, freedom, and cooperation, but let's not think that we can or should control every aspect of a person's life.

THE UNIVERSAL LAWS

Paul: So how do we create schools, churches and other institutions that help us individuate in a way that respects the needs of other people?

Jesus: Well, Moses told you one way. He said "don't kill each other."

He didn't say you all needed to study Algebra. He didn't say you all needed to read the Talmud. He didn't say that capitalism is better than communism. He just said "don't kill each other."

Yet somehow the Jew thinks he has to kill the Muslim and the Muslim thinks he has to kill the Jew. People commit murder and then the State thinks it has the right to execute them. People have all kinds of reasons why they think killing is necessary.

Yet God didn't say to the Jewish people "Don't kill, except in special circumstances." He said "don't kill" period. End of sentence. But people added on their own sentences. And before you know it, killing was acceptable. Right now, in Israel, Jews and Palestinians are killing each other.

Are Jews obeying the laws of Moses? Are Arabs obeying the teachings of Muhammad?

Is there any place on earth where this single commandment against killing is being kept? What good are laws if no one follows them?

I have news for you . . . if you are really a Jew, a Christian, a Muslim, a Buddhist or a Hindu you cannot kill. Because the commandment against killing is a core element of any authentic spiritual teaching. You will find similar teachings about "not stealing" because these are universal behavioral norms. To ask this much of people is reasonable in any culture. It provides protection for people without unreasonably restricting their freedom.

There are certain laws—and there aren't many—that need to be energetically enforced so that people are safe and free to pursue their happiness. But when society reaches beyond this to control the lives of people, it builds a prison that will eventually have to be destroyed.

BUILDING A HUMANE AND JUST SOCIETY

Paul: You seem to be in favor of only the most basic social limits on the freedom of individuals, particularly those laws and rules that guard the people's safety.

Jesus: Yes, that is correct. However, when you translate the latter part of that statement into human terms, you will see that it is a lot bigger than you think. For example, I don't believe that anyone who is forced to go without food, housing or medical care has the safety s/he requires to prosper as a human being.

In a country where people are committed to sharing these resources, there is no reason for government to intervene. However, in a country where people are hungry, homeless, or sick, society has a responsibility to help.

Yet such help should empower people to take responsibility for their lives if they are able to. It should not make people dependent on others, because dependence does not foster human growth and development.

To put it simply, the laws and agreements of society should foster an environment in which individuals can grow and express themselves without hurting others or infringing on their rights.

When people know how to live and let live, there is no need for outside regulation of human affairs. Self-regulation is the best and most efficient form of government so long as it is guided by the golden rule (do unto others as you would have them do unto you).

A just society is created not from the top down, but from the bottom up. When each individual acts with fairness toward others and accepts no less in return, justice is created in the body politic.

Society is as good as the individuals that make it up. That is why the work of social transformation must happen in the trenches, not in the boardrooms. Hope, trust and faith must be established and measured one person at a time.

TEACHERS AND MIRACLES

Paul: A lot of what you say makes sense to me. But is it possible that someone else may feel closer to another teacher?

Jesus: Yes, some can learn better from another teacher, whether in our tradition or in a different tradition.

Consciousness is infinitely varied. Some minds are on one wavelength and others are on a different one. I encourage people to explore the options until they find a teacher and a tradition that speaks to them.

Paul: Do all of us need a teacher?

Jesus: No. You do not need a teacher. Life is the best teacher, but there will be times when you are confused or in pain and you will ask for help. When that happens, help will come to you in a form that is understandable to you.

Paul: Does our call for help bring miracles to us?

Jesus: It may or it may not. Miracles are not understandable to any of us. They happen, but we do not know why or how. They are part of the mystery.

You can participate in a miracle by being willing to do your part, but you cannot make miracles happen at will. No one can.

Paul: Did you not make miracles?

Jesus: I participated in a number of miraculous events, but those miracles were made by God, not by me.

Miracles are the laws of God asserting themselves. We are blessed when we can assist in the process. But as soon as we think that we are the ones doing it, we cease being instruments of divine grace.

Paul: So we can participate in miraculous events?

Jesus: Yes. You can be a vehicle for the expression of God's love in the world just as I am. You just need to be willing.

If you accept God's Will for you then you can become a vehicle for the expression of that Will. And only that surrender on your part can bring genuine happiness into your life.

BEING A MINISTER OF LOVE

Paul: Once that happiness comes into your life you want to share it with others, do you not?

Jesus: Yes, and by then you know that you are worthy of the trust He has placed in you. And you are not afraid to stand up and be His hands and His feet, and His voice in the world. And so your words will reach out to others as my words have reached out to you, for you too will become a way-shower.

After all, there is no less pain today than there was in my

time. The same voices of fear are heard in the land. Brother still stands against brother and in the name of some love made special both are slain.

Since you are there in your world and I am not, it is only through you that my ministry of love goes forward.

Paul: What do you ask of us?

Jesus: I ask you to commit to the truth within your heart and to be willing to share that truth whenever the occasion arises.

Those who are lost cannot save themselves for they do not know that they have strayed from the fold. The flock has broken through the boundaries erected for its safety and so the shepherd must be sent forth in search of it. And you who have strayed from the fold and found your way back home understand these wayward ones as I once understood you.

Thus, your time has come to minister to the truth which brought you home. Many who are thirsty for the truth await your footsteps. Go to them now, as I came to you.

I have offered you my torn mantle . . . take a piece of it and go forth. Comfort those who are broken and bereft. As they find faith in you, their faith in me shall be renewed and together we will approach the God who made us as equals and loves us all the same.

It is through me that you will return to God because I understand you. And you in turn will offer others the same understanding and compassion.

You will be the doorway for others just I was the doorway for you. That is the way the teaching is passed on.

HONORING THE EXPERIENCE OF OTHERS

Paul: Sometimes it seems to me that you speak like a missionary and other times it seems that the cornerstone of your teaching is giving people the space to have their own experiences and make up their own minds. How do you reconcile the two?

Jesus: When you find something that helps you, it is natural to want to share this with others. But there is a correct way to do this and an incorrect way. The correct way honors the experience of others and allows for the possibility that their experience may be different from yours. The incorrect way seeks to impose your experience on others and does not allow for the possibility that they may benefit from another teaching or approach.

To be mute because you may offend others does not facilitate the telling of truth. To claim to have the only correct belief and be overbearing in professing it does not facilitate the telling of truth either.

The first stance is cowardly. The second stance is tyrannical

An authentic person is neither a coward nor a tyrant. He shares his own experience openly while respecting the experience of others. He is not afraid to witness to the ideas that have helped him, nor is he afraid to admit that his experience may be different from the experience of others. He knows that one man's wine can be another's poison. Therefore, he offers his cup to others respectfully, encouraging them to drink only if they feel comfortable doing so.

His approach is simple. He says to others: "I have found these shoes to be very comfortable. They have helped me walk on my journey. If they fit you, please feel free to walk in them. If they don't, please don't try to make them fit. Wait for a pair of shoes that fit you." He knows the universe will provide the right shoes when the aspirant is ready to embark on his or her journey.

He knows that truth takes many forms and each one of those forms is necessary. Therefore, he does not argue with the form, but sees and affirms the content.

Paul: You are asking us to be very broadminded in the way that we hold our truth, but not to be afraid to share it with others.

Jesus: Right. Sharing truth is important. How else does it reach to those who thirst for it?

But imposing your version of truth on another is simple trespass. There is no excuse for it.

Consider this simple analogy. Your favorite fruit is a green apple. You love the tart, sweet taste. So when you pass by the orchard, you pick as many apples as you can hold in your pocket.

Then you see your friend approaching you on the road and you get very excited. "How wonderful," you think. "I will give him one of my apples and he will love it."

So you greet your friend and offer him your nicest looking apple. And he can see your excitement and he doesn't want to disappoint you, even though he is not crazy about apples. So he takes a bite and thanks you for your gift, which he quickly puts into his pocket. "I will finish eating it later," he tells you. I am not very hungry now."

Do you respect your friend's desires and his experience or do you feel rebuffed because he did not respond to your offer with the same enthusiasm you had in making it? Do you want him to eat the apple even though he may not enjoy it? What if he is allergic to apples? Do you still want him to eat it?

How far will you go to impose your experience on him?

Remember now, that apple can be anything. It can be a book or a piece of music that you like. It could be a political or religious idea.

Will you judge him because he doesn't like your apple? Will you spread false rumors about him? Will you put him on trial and convict him of crimes he did not commit? How far will you go to try and make him accept your experience, your ideas, your values?

I assure you that human beings have condemned one another to die for no other reason than that they preferred peaches to apples.

Is that the way you express your truth?

I have told you many times to let those who like apples eat apples and those who like peaches eat peaches. One group is not better than the other.

Moreover, please let those who like peaches proclaim the benefits of eating peaches and let those who like eating apples proclaim the benefits of eating apples. That is their right.

It may be that each side will exaggerate the benefits of their chosen fruit and exaggerate the dangers of the other fruit. Such exaggeration is unfortunate, but it is hardly a reason to silence either side.

In the end, people will have to have their own experience and make up their own minds. Some will try apples and spit them out. Others will devour them with a passion. Peaches will have similar demographics.

There is no greater system than the one that gives people all of the information available and then grants them the freedom to make up their own minds. That is true in business. It is true in government. And it is true in the ministry.

Share your information but do not preach unless you are invited to. And do not try to convert others, but encourage them to make up their own minds.

If you can do this, then you will neither be a coward nor a tyrant. You will stand up for your truth and respect the experience of others.

Truth that is neither spoken nor embodied in acts does not reach out to people. It has no power to transform lives.

But truth that is embellished and over-promoted will sound hollow because it is. It lacks integrity and people can feel it.

THE PRICE OF PROTECTION

Paul: Do you think people can always detect fraud? "Buyer beware" is a policy that works for smart people who can separate the wheat from the chaff, but it does not work particularly well for those who cannot tell the difference between the two. Shouldn't there be some protection for people who are easily manipulated or fooled?

Jesus: Well, in certain circumstances this might seem like a good idea, but what is the price that you pay once you have an outside authority making decisions for you? If you let religion or government separate the wheat from the chaff for you, what happens when they act in bad faith and start giving you chaff and calling it "wheat?"

You think you need them to protect you from unscrupulous people, but who will protect you from them if they become unscrupulous?

Now you may be too lazy to read the latest consumer studies, but do you really want an outside authority deciding what is good for your health and well-being. Isn't that a responsibility you want to keep for yourself?

Do you want state religion, state medicine and state education or do you want to choose your own spiritual orientation, approach to health care for your family, and education for your children?

Do you want to choose, or would you prefer to have someone else choose for you? This is the simple decision that humankind faces today. Either you move toward greater individual responsibility and self-regulation or you move toward greater outside control from authority figures and the systems they represent.

Do you want your church, your government, your school saying "no more apples; we will serve only oranges from now on" or do you want to make that choice yourself?

Don't be stupid about this. Unless you are willing to take responsibility for your life and educate yourself to make the key decisions that face you, you will give your power away. And does it matter to whom you give it? Is it any better to give it to the church than to the government?

If you think so, you are in for a very rude awakening. No form of religious or secular authority protects the rights of individuals to choose for themselves. All forms of outward authority seek primarily to perpetuate themselves.

Paul: Well, it is easier to give the responsibility away than it is to keep it. If we keep it, we might have to stop blaming each other and find a way to get along.

Jesus: That's true. Besides, no outside authority is going to make you love each other and learn to cooperate. This is something you have to learn to do on your own.

Life teaches you that when you try to take any advantage of another, you withhold freedom from yourself. What you try to manipulate will not submit to you, except by force. And the more you "force" life, the less chance you have of experiencing creativity and grace—the gifts of your divinity.

Ironically, God would gladly and gracefully give you what you try to take for yourself and subsequently lose in the struggle. You think you know what you need, but God knows what you need far better than you do.

It is indeed a paradox. If you want to experience the joy and freedom that has been promised to you, you must submit your will to a Greater will than the one that is attached to your ego structure.

No, it is not the will of church or state. It is not the will of other men or women. It is the Will of the life force itself whose primary purpose is love.

A SERVANT OF LOVE

Jesus: You must become a servant of Love to be granted the greatest creative freedom. For when you serve love you care for others as well as yourself. You serve the greater good and so you too benefit, in ways you cannot know.

The servant of love does not ask "What about me?" because s/he knows that what benefits the whole must benefit every part. It is inconceivable that those who offer caring and love to others could receive anything less than that back. For love increases as it is given and received.

God's increase does not seek to benefit any one part at the expense of another. And so all prosper together.

I will tell you very simply what you need to know. You cannot benefit yourself alone. To try to do so is to flounder and fail.

Take care of yourself but keep the good of others in your thoughts and prayers, because what you offer them will surely come to you, as if you wished for it directly.

God did not create you separately but "of one piece." Each one of you is part of the fabric of humanity. No matter how hard you try to escape this, you will be brought back to it in the end. Your good and that of your brother and sister are one and the same. This was true at the moment of your creation and it is still true now.

Yet understand, your duty to humanity is not to try to be like others, but to be yourself and to encourage others to be themselves. You cannot force another person to be kind and loving. You cannot compel honesty or fairness. It must develop spontaneously in each heart. And what helps it develop is simple support and encouragement of the creative process within each person.

Support the other person in being who he is and it will not be hard for him to love you. Indeed, by encouraging him to be himself you are teaching him how to love others without conditions. And he will learn to give to others the support you gave to him.

Society cannot be regulated from the top down. Hierarchical powers cannot empower but only oppress. True empowerment happens from the bottom up, from one individual encouraging another. Love given as a gift will give itself again and again.

This is my ministry. It is a ministry of love, not coercion. It shares but does not browbeat or insist. It does not seek to limit or control others, but trusts people to make the choices that are best for them. It is an open hand extended, not a closed fist.

Of course, as soon as the religion of love is proclaimed, someone arrives carrying a sword and announcing the next Crusade.

I ask you to leave me out of all that. I do not want to try to cram my love down anyone's throat.

Mine is a far more gentle and trusting way. You know it comes from me because the love it proclaims is offered in a loving way. If it is not offered in a loving way, it does not come from me, but from the fears of the one who refuses to trust you to decide for yourself.

Part Three

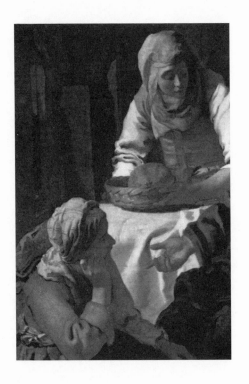

Questions for Paul

ALL OUR ILLUSIONS WILL BE DESTROYED

Ricardo: I have been a recovering alcoholic since 1992. In early 1996 I became severely depressed. Though I was following all the suggestions of the AA program, my life, which had improved greatly after twenty-eight years of full blown alcoholism, started to crumble all over again. I even became suicidal for a while.

I decided to move to a new town where I had gone for treatment in 1992. It was a real soul-searching mission. I decided to attempt college and become a Substance Abuse Counselor. During my first semester, I shocked myself by making the Honor Roll. Then, I started to question my motives. Was this an ego trip? Was I avoiding my issues in my home state?

It was at this time that I came across your book *Love Without Conditions.* Once I started reading, I couldn't put it down. It was as if a light went off. *Silence of the Heart* came out right after that and it felt like you were writing to me. I had never read any books on spirituality prior to this and it was scary to me.

I made the Dean's List the next three semesters and graduated college. I took a job as a counselor and then the opportunity to open my own treatment center appeared. I worked very hard and got the center open and thought I had found my path. However, that was not the case. Six months later I was forced to close the center for reasons beyond my control.

It was as if someone had torn my heart out, and I have been struggling emotionally ever since. I even relapsed seven months ago and have had difficulty deciding what direction I should take. I just feel very alone and confused about my path in life. Do you have any suggestions?

Paul: Well, Ricardo, we must never measure our success in life based on the external situations that present themselves. True success is found in our ability to be loving toward ourselves and others. It is not found in being rich and famous, or in having a great treatment center.

All external situations change. If we are attached to them, we suffer when things shift. Jesus said we are to find our treasure in our hearts, not in the world.

He asked us to be in the world, but not of the world. That means that we do what we can do with integrity and leave the rest to God. We can't be attached to the outcome.

Like Job, we can learn to be close to God even when the jewels of this world are being taken away from us. Letting go of what does not truly belong to us or to what we no longer need lightens our burden and enables us to dive deeper into our spiritual lives.

Sometimes, when we invite God into our lives, S/he seems to enter quite ruthlessly and our whole life appears to be a shambles. God is not just Vishnu, the preserver, but also Shiva, the destroyer. It seems that all our illusions must be destroyed if we are to embrace truth fully.

To give up on yourself because the external form in your life is changing is to miss the lesson of your alcoholism. The real substance is within. It is not in a bottle, nor is it in a posh treatment center.

Love is what nurtures and sustains. Everything else is an illusion. Welcome to the spiritual path, brother.

This is probably not the last time life will play a few tricks on you. But whatever happens, hold onto love, for yourself and others. It is your life raft through the stormy waters.

SHARING OUR FEELINGS
WITH OUR PARTNER

Sondra: I am in a new relationship and my partner wants me to express my fears to him. I am sometimes reluctant because I am afraid to show my vulnerability and the depth of my fears. Is it better to express our feelings or is it better to keep these feelings to ourselves?

Paul: This is a good question. I think it is important to find a balance between sharing our fears with our partner and taking responsibility for riding them out on our own.

If we share every fear, we can put our partner through an emotional buzz saw. That puts a big strain on the relationship. Better to ride out some of these emotional vacillations on our own. Then, when we really need our partner's attention, we can ask for it legitimately.

On the other hand, if we have fears that keep coming up, then we need to share them or we are withholding important information from our partner. And that would be a retreat from intimacy.

LESSONS IN LOVE AT AN EARLY AGE

Veronica: We have a lovely eight year old who has a lot of social difficulties—kids picking on her, groups ostracizing her for being different than they are—and she is really sensitive and wants friends very much. She does okay with some children, one on one, but invariably in group situations she becomes the scapegoat. If they tease her she cries and then they increase the teasing.

169

She is beautiful and intelligent and verbally precocious, and adults love her, but she wants friends her own age. We teach her ideas about God's love for her and let her know that other kids' judgments about her have much more to do with them than with her, but it is still difficult for her.

Any insights or ideas we could share with her?

Paul: Jesus said "love your enemies." He also said "turn the other cheek." I guess your daughter is being asked to practice the master's teaching at an early age!

Tell her not to hold back her love even though other people are unkind. In time, even the hardest hearts melt in the face of devoted and persistent love. Jesus loved that way and he asked us to do so too.

It's easy to love when other people love us back. It's not so easy when they don't. Tell your daughter that God has given her a big challenge. Chances are He wouldn't have given her this challenge if she wasn't up to it!

NO VICARIOUS ATONEMENT

Deborah: A friend lent me your tape on unconditional love. At one point you say Jesus did not die for our sins. If so, then why did he die on the cross? Why did he go through all of that pain and suffering and why is he called the Redeemer? I deeply connected to everything else on the tapes, but this threw me a bit of a curve.

Paul: There is no vicarious atonement. Jesus knows this better than anyone. Each one of us must atone. Each one of us must choose to come back into alignment with the divine will. If Jesus could have done this for us, we would not be here now. The fact that we are here suggests that we all have this work to do.

Jesus is a model, a way-shower. He shows us what we can and must accomplish. His crucifixion and resurrection was not our release, but his. Each one of us must recognize our innocence and that of all of our brothers and sisters, just as Jesus did.

Alignment and atonement are and must forever be up to us. That is the meaning of free will, which is the keynote of our embodiment here.

FREEDOM TO CHOOSE OR TO COMPLY

Miguel: I am having difficulty in reconciling the apparent contradiction between the concept of freedom of choice and the Universal Law of Karma. If we truly had freedom, there would not be predetermined effects or consequences. The law of Karma suggests that we are only truly free when we think and act in accordance with Universal Law of God. To me, this is not freedom; it is compliance. Why don't they just call it the Universal Law of Compliance! It seems that the only freedom we have is in determining how long we postpone our inevitable compliance with Universal Law.

I grew up with the fundamentalists telling me that I HAD TO accept Jesus Christ as my Lord and Savior or else be eternally damned. Now I have the New Thought/New Age teachings saying that as long as we choose to postpone our assent into Higher Consciousness we must endure the "negative" consequences. Is there any real difference in these teachings?

171

Paul: Great question!

We have the freedom to choose the way we want to think and act and, yes, we reap the results of what we sow. However, this does not happen in any kind of linear way. Hence, some people who do all the right things still get cancer and die and some people who kill and rape seem to get away without consequences.

God doesn't have a police force or even a hit squad, so if you or anyone else wants revenge you'll be sadly disappointed. And, I'm sorry to say, if you are looking for justice (an eye for an eye), you'll be a bit disgruntled too.

But if you look at things in the long haul, you see that our thinking and the actions that arise from them eventually catch up to us. A wolf just isn't happy wearing sheep's clothes forever. So whatever is in your mind will eventually come out. You can't hide it indefinitely.

And then you have to look at it and see whether or not it is contributing to your happiness. And if it isn't, you have a chance to change it. Life is generous and gracious in this way. It gives us many opportunities to end our suffering.

Do you have free will? Of course you do. You can keep saying "no" to love and you can keep your pain alive. Are you likely to do this? Well, everyone has a limit as to how much pain is enough.

So, yes, the outcome is in a way guaranteed. You might even say that the deck is stacked. Chances are very strong that you will choose love, sooner or later.

Whether it will be sooner or later is up to you. And please remember, even if you decide to choose love right now, it doesn't mean that you will get a new Mercedes.

The choice is a deeper one than most new age pundits know,

because it's not just the spiritual adult who must choose, but also the wounded child who isn't sure he is worthy of love. Believe me, there's enough challenge here to keep us all busy for a while.

If you don't believe me and you believe the pundits of angel glitter, why not just click your shoes together like Dorothy and go right to Oz. (I tried this when I was five and it didn't work. But you never know, maybe it will work for you.)

Now for the tough part: it is possible to love Jesus and hate his brothers and sisters . . . an incongruency that keeps cropping up in the bible-thumping, born-again, instant oatmeal approach to salvation. Oh well, Jesus didn't tell us he'd love our enemies for us. He told us we would have to learn to do it. And so we all got homework.

What's wrong, you don't like the assignment?

Not many people do, no matter which side of the theological aisle they sit on!

HIDING OUR PAIN VS TELLING THE TRUTH

Cindy: I am grappling with whether I have truly let go of a lot of pain in my life or whether I am masking it with kindness to others.

It seems that when I am in the state of pain, I become more giving and loving to others. Sometimes this brings creative and beautiful results. When my mom had sudden open-heart surgery two weeks after she and I had a big breakup, I felt a sense of peace and love that was so euphoric. I had complete forgiveness in my heart.

But sometimes, I fall into a trap. Some of my friends can't

seem to live with me being peaceful or loving to them and I become unbelievably entangled in a drama that results in me eventually cutting them off after they push me to the brink. It's as if I suddenly wake up from a dream and am in a nightmare.

For the past nine months, I have been trying to assess if I am doing this from low self esteem (or the martyr complex from Roman Catholic days). Any ideas?

Paul: Masking pain isn't usually such a good idea. Better to be up front about what you are feeling. When you pretend to be okay and you're not, you invite people to continue the same behavior toward you that may be causing you pain. Honesty is the best policy, even though it is sometimes difficult.

Perhaps you think that by telling people how you feel you will offend them and lose their love. Not wanting to risk that, you remain silent. Then people interpret your silence as a license to continue until you feel "pushed to the brink."

But please realize that they are pushing only because you are not telling them to stop. In that sense, your behavior is encouraging theirs.

The irony is that by "cutting them off" you lose their love anyway. So the very situation you sought to avoid by withholding the truth you actually end up creating.

When you understand this self-destructive pattern, you can begin to reverse it by speaking up in the beginning. Then, you and your friends can negotiate what feels good to both of you, so that no one has to cut anyone off.

Telling the truth in a loving and respectful way creates awareness and understanding. Don't be afraid to do it.

NOT KNOWING WHERE TO GO

Richard: I have been on the planet for 52 years, knew from very young I was gay, grew up in a violent abusive family. I went through Vietnam as a CO, took care of burns, became a drunk like many in my family and went through recovery with the 12 Steps. I went into the seminary after taking care of many who died from AIDS, then left the seminary to take care of my father as he died from alcoholism. I stayed with my mother for as long as I could, drank again, got sober again, went back to graduate school in psychology and theology and now understand more. Even though I live in the Bay Area, I still witness the hatred toward gay people and much of the time I don't feel much of a bond with other gay people.

I feel driven to find that very personal Jesus. I worked with children and families in a school setting, intervening in domestic and school problems, and that was a true grace. Children brought me back to myself and helped me find some things I had lost over the years. Now I work for some lawyers during the day and go to school at night. The only reason I work there is because there is one boss who loves God; yet he is homophobic.

I thought about going back to the seminary to serve those on the margin but they decided that even though I am now sober a long time they don't want me back because of "the centrality of the Eucharist."

I am discussing your books with a friend of mine who has been in AA for 25 years. I resonate with a great deal of your material. I feel I am going away from Catholicism, although I don't know where to go. I feel beat up by religion.

As your head grays and you know for sure you will die, those little props religion offers you begin to fall through. I am not sure where to turn or how to find my path. Yet I feel that this is somehow pleasing to God.

Paul: I am certain that you will find your path, as you have done all your life. Don't be concerned that your path is not like that of others. It takes courage to be yourself and not live in reaction to the likes and dislikes of others. As long as you stay in your heart and deepen in your love for yourself and others, it does not matter where you go or what you do. Indeed, as you surrender the need to figure things out in advance, the doors will open to you spontaneously when it is time.

BREATHING DEEPLY

Jenn: I wanted to ask you a question about breathing. In reading your book *Silence of the Heart,* you described breathing deeply every moment. I have found this technique very useful. Initially, I used it only in my quiet times. But now, I am ready to move on and incorporate it into my whole life. I have found that this breathing technique is very effective in interacting with people, as it melts away ego and related emotional reactivity so that I can see the person (or people) in front of me for who they truly are. However, there is one area in which I have difficulty incorporating the breathing exercise. As a scientist, I read a lot of analytical material and I find it difficult to incorporate the breath while reading this kind of material. When I'm in that state associated with the breathing, I find it difficult to focus, learn and absorb scientific material. Would you have any suggestions on how to maintain and/or enhance the ability to absorb scientific material while I maintain the breath?

Paul: The purpose of this type of breathing is to go beyond the mind that reads scientific papers. If you want to improve comprehension of scientific papers, try a quick walk or run around the block, or some fast breathing.

THE TRUTH OF OTHERS

Iris: In the past couple of weeks I have been through a very intense time. I have been through two relationships, one male and the other female, and both relationships didn't last. I was sexually abused as a child and, as a result, I often sleep with men the first day I meet them, even though I don't really want to. Because I don't speak my truth, I give my power away and don't respect my body.

Now I've decided to make a different choice, but that doesn't heal the darkness I carry inside of me. I've been listening to other people's truths and it's been driving me nuts! One teacher says, "What power? That's only a mind thing." My other teacher tells me "you have to empty the cup first before it can be refilled, and I say, "how do I empty it to let the love in?" I'm so confused, can you help me?

Paul: The first law of love is to be gentle with yourself. If you will make that your absolute number one priority, the rest will follow.

Being gentle with yourself does not mean doing what others want you to do when you don't want to do it. It means honoring the part of you that says "no." When you can do that, you can say "no" to others and they will believe you. You can't attract what you want into your life until you say "no" to what you don't want.

Be patient. It might not happen overnight, but it will happen if you learn to listen to yourself. In that respect, don't accept teachings from others, including from me, if they are not the teachings of your own heart.

SELF-ACCEPTANCE IS EVERY DAY SPIRITUAL PRACTICE

Louise: For most of my life I have struggled with accepting myself and God. I do not think that I have ever truly experienced my own self worth, though I have tried to establish it in so many ways.

When reading *A Course in Miracles* and related books, I yearn for some reminder of who I am. I know and understand completely that I cannot truly offer love, acceptance and forgiveness to others without first loving myself, but how do I do that? I see how clingy I become in my relationships when I feel no self worth, how judgmental I become with others when I am viciously judging myself, and I lose complete presence. I am very sad. I know in my heart that I am missing a lot. Yet I want only to know love. I want only to shine so that I can invite others to shine too.

I understand that there is only love and fear, but fear seems to speak so loudly and so emphatically. Where is God? Is He waiting on me or shall I wait on Him? Am I so afraid of love that I cannot receive it?

I have broken myself down into so many tiny pieces trying to understand all this, but all I seem to be left with are words and a blaring ego. If God is here and his love surrounds me always, why can't I feel it? How can I make myself love myself?

Paul: As you know, Louise, it all begins with you. Yet you cannot "make" yourself love yourself, just as you cannot make yourself love others. Love begins with simple acceptance. It is "simple" to understand, but not at all easy to do.

Sometimes it is helpful to start by being aware of the times when you are being critical of yourself and others. Just be aware . . . don't beat yourself . . . and then practice compassion for yourself. See that you are being critical and that means you are scared. Allow yourself to feel some compassion for the little girl who is scared.

Accepting yourself in each moment is spiritual work. It is an ongoing practice. Unfortunately, there are no shortcuts.

Love follows on the "heals" of acceptance. And God's love for you follows on your love and acceptance of yourself.

Reading books may help you understand what the scope of the journey is, but they don't walk it for you.

You talk about wanting "to shine." If you haven't seen the movie *Shine,* please do so. It gives a great road map for becoming an authentic person and encouraging others to do the same.

By the way, the words that you write are not just your words. They are everyone's words. We are all working the same material here.

DANGERS OF NOT BREATHING

Gayle: I am experiencing now a fear of sickness and death. Every time I get sick my mind says that I'm going to die and this is something that happens to me over and over again.

Sometimes I wonder if my fear is actually creating my illness. I don't know when to pay attention to my fear or when to say that it's just phony baloney.

I'm really tired of all this. Sometimes, I feel like I can't breathe or swallow without it hurting (literally and figuratively). I don't want to feel like I have to push breath into my lungs.

Paul: Not breathing is a sign of overwhelm, an attempt to escape the fear, rather than be with it.

When fear comes up, the breath becomes short and labored.

It is good to be aware of this and to take long deep breaths when the fear begins. As you breathe, just be aware of what you are thinking and feeling. If you stay with this long enough, you may be less overwhelmed.

In other words, you use the breathing to establish a place of peace from which you can begin to be with your thoughts and feelings so that you can accept them, learn from them, and move with them.

Then fear will no longer hold you back. It will become a doorway you can walk through.

As always, be gentle with yourself. Do not force yourself to do anything you are not ready to do.

ONE PERSON'S DESERT
IS ANOTHER'S POISON

Lila: As a breatharian, I have for a long time believed that food is a drug or a poison. It is the reason we get sick and it causes all pain and suffering. I am consumed with this UNDERSTAND-ING, but still have doubts, even though I see the reversal of aging and its effects when I go towards fruit, water etc. What does Jesus say on this?

Is Jesus God? Is breatharian the new heaven with no death, no suffering, no tears?

Paul: If Jesus is God, then so are you, and you will find the answers to your questions within your own consciousness. Neither Jesus nor I has some special authority to tell you what is good for you.

As for breatharian: beware of absolutes. They are much more poisonous than any food substance!

Food, like anything else, is relative. One man's desert is another man's poison.

If you listen to your body, it will tell you what kind of food works best for you.

THE NEXT BUDDHA OR CHRIST

Thomas: I love your books and find a lot of correspondences to the writings of Matthew Fox, which I also love. In his book *The Coming Of The Cosmic Christ,* Matthew Fox speaks of the "wounded child" in us all which he equates with the crucified earth on the one hand and the Cosmic Christ on the other. The

Cosmic Christ is also sometimes identified with the Buddha Maitreya. It is believed by some that Maitreya is currently living in London and waiting for the right moment to reveal himself.

What's been puzzling me and what your book *Silence Of The Heart* helped answer concerns the fact that some evangelical Christians consider Maitreya to be the Antichrist. While I consider this to be an extreme point of view, I also believe that all views deserve some respect. Anyway, I'd been looking for a way that could perhaps synthesize the views of Maitreya and his followers with those of Matthew Fox. *Silence Of The Heart* came to the rescue when it equated the "wounded child" with Lucifer and the Antichrist. As a "wounded child" myself, this has helped me on a personal level to accept and integrate my "dark" side without feeling that I am being false to God or Jesus in doing so. Thank you very much.

Paul: If Maitreya is either Christ or AntiChrist, then it makes him very special, does it not? And he isn't special, any more than Jesus, or Krishnamurti, who was heralded as the next incarnation of Buddha just a generation ago, or you or me.

Christ is not a person, but a state of consciousness (as is anti-Christ) and no one has exclusive claim to either one.

Only the Jews seem to understand that the Messiah does not come until all beings return to God. No exceptions.

And, while the possibility of the Messiah returning is ever-present, don't hold your breath! Besides, breathing is good for all of us!

RECEIVING MESSAGES FROM SPIRIT

Annada: For about a year I have been having thoughts in my mind that do not seem to be the same as the thoughts that I normally have. They are difficult to describe. They seem to be from a source that thinks of Itself as God. The messages come when I can manage to keep my mind an absolute blank. I am not at all aware of where the message is headed and it is as big a surprise to me when I hear it, as it would be to anyone reading an unfamiliar passage in a book for the first time. If I start to think what is going to come next, the thoughts instantly go away. When I clear my mind, they are back. They often come with the strong urge to write them down. At first I thought that I was losing my mind, and I became very frightened. From my German, Catholic upbringing I had always been told that people who claimed to have these types of experiences were either liars, or they were crazy.

I took copies of the writings to a psychiatrist, two psychologists, and a Catholic priest, fully expecting to be medicated out of whatever was happening to me. To my surprise, none of them told me I was crazy, or even that I was imagining the things that I had written. They each had a little different idea about what was happening.

I don't know what to think. If I am somehow making this all up, it is certainly on a subconscious level. I have no basis from which to determine if some of the things I have written are true or not, although I have written nothing that I know isn't true. I have been a bit hesitant to share this material because of my confusion about it. I would be appalled if I ever did anything to mislead anyone about something this important.

Please give me your opinion as I have complete confidence in you after reading some of your material.

Paul: No, Annada. None of this sounds crazy. Going into the silence and hearing the truth are the essential activities of this spiritual path. That is what all of the prophets did. And that is what many inspired writers, teachers, and spiritual men and women have done throughout history.

It is not surprising that you hear the truth. Indeed, it would be surprising—if your heart and mind are open—if you didn't hear the truth. Of course, not everyone has the experience of bringing information through as you describe. So it may be that this is a gift that has been given to you and, if so, it is important to share this gift with others.

As for misleading others, remember that messages from the One Essence are always uplifting, inspiring, centering, encouraging. They do not confuse, baffle, or make it more difficult for us to live a simple, fulfilled life, loving ourselves and others. This is the true goal. If the messages you receive contribute in this positive way, then you are blessed indeed and so are the people you share them with.

DEALING WITH GUILT

Eva: Recently I hurt someone in my life. I have since apologized to that person. I recognize that the part of me that attacked is the part of me that doesn't feel loveable. I know that it's a matter of me forgiving myself and loving that part of me that feels unlovable.

Even with the above recognition, I am still feeling guilty.

Any words on really letting go of the guilt?

Paul: You can start by holding your guilt or discomfort in a compassionate way. Stop beating yourself up for feeling guilty or not forgiving yourself totally. Just see what's there and acknowledge it.

The more conscious you become in this moment, the less possibility for betraying yourself or others. As you learn to bring love and acceptance to yourself now, the past becomes less and less significant and can simply be viewed as a training ground. Or as the I Ching says: No praise, no blame.

THE MORE COOKS THE MERRIER

George: I read only a few pages in your book entitled *Love Without Conditions* and it began to change my life. What was said within those pages impacted me strongly. Perhaps I was ready to listen again. The words were not foreign to me. I had read them many times, yet somehow something was conveyed to me emotionally and I have started to change for the better.

I look at it as a stepping stone in my life. The first time this happened to me was when I read the works of Swami Vivekananda. That was about 10 years ago. Ever since then, I was waiting for the next step.

Your book made it happen. I feel like I am only on the beginning stages of what's unfolding within me and I am excited about it. I think I am finally ready to surrender to the Christ or God within me.

Paul: The fact that you responded in this way to both

Vivekananda's words and my words demonstrates how unique each one of our spiritual journeys is. We always find the teaching we need when we are ready.

What goes into your pot might not go into someone else's and vice versa, but everybody I ever met who was exploring in earnest was making some kind of "soup" or "stew." Usually there was more than one ingredient, not to mention the variety of spices chosen.

I think that the churches and temples of the 21st century will eventually realize this and start offering cooking classes. I'm one of those people that thinks "the more cooks the merrier."

Cable Television seems to agree. Now, Julia Child is not the only chef preaching about "the joy of cooking."

Anyway, welcome to our cookclub. Maybe one day I'll see you on TV putting a little Vivekananda into the stew!

A BLESSING FOR THE NEW YEAR

Laura: I wanted to thank you for e-mailing me back. I really appreciate that. You are there helping many who are yearning for change in their lives.

I am a 20 year old female really wanting to live my life in love and express my truth. I am doing that now, but I feel very uncomfortable with all the changes that are taking place. I feel like something or someone is stepping inside my body and turning everything around. It's horrible, but it's also beautiful.

I always knew that there was another kind of love which I feel was never given to me by my parents or society and I know that I am that love.

Paul: Since you know that you are this love that you want to give and receive, you have the most important piece of knowledge available to you. It is the Holy Grail people go around the world seeking, looking everywhere except within their own hearts and minds.

This priceless knowledge will steer you away from hundreds of cul de sacs, aborted promises and shortcuts that never materialize. What a great way to begin the new year knowing that the Source of love is within yourself! May we all celebrate that knowledge and remember it every day during the coming year.

HUMPY DUMPTY'S OFF THE WALL AGAIN

Gwen: I've been going through a lot lately in my life and I am so confused. It's like "wham," one lesson after the other, and I've been breathing and feeling my feelings, but it is just too intense for me. I feel like I can't handle it anymore.

I recently told a friend of mine that he was being too demanding of me. For a long time I didn't communicate my feelings to him because he took everything so seriously. But this time I got really upset and I told him in a stern voice "I can't respond to your demands for love. I'm putting you before myself. Please, I just want to be alone right now."

I feel guilty now for talking to him that way because he said I was being completely abusive. But I feel like I abused myself by being too scared to speak up. And now I'm wondering why I keep creating all this drama in my life. I want to lock myself in my house and never come out. I'm completely embarrassed!

I do all of this spiritual reading to better my life, but I feel like I keep making bad choices. I'm tired of feeling bad about myself and my relationships. I'm wondering what I'm doing wrong?

Paul: I think you need to realize that this is a chance to be more honest with yourself and understand the cycle of pain you are locked into. Here's how it looks from the outside in:

1. You don't want to do something, but you do it anyway because you want to be accepted by others.

2. You resent doing it, but you keep doing it until the self-betrayal is so extreme you can't stand it anymore.

3. You explode, project blame onto the other person, and say "I can't respond to your demands for love."

Now, if you are tired of this, you can get off the wheel of your pain. Here's how.

Do things because you want to do them, not because someone else expects you to do them or because you are trying to "buy" their acceptance or love. When you don't want to do something, say "no" gently but clearly. Ambivalence here leads into the scenario of self-betrayal and inappropriate blame described above. A simple "no" said clearly from the heart can prevent the drama of self-abuse.

Others who are drawn into our dramas have their own lessons in this area, but it is pointless to try to teach them or correct them. We need to address our own issues.

When we no longer betray ourselves, we will no longer attract people we betray or who betray us. It's time that we begin to realize that the crime and the punishment for self-betrayal belong to us. And we are free to stop punishing ourselves at any time. When the pain becomes great enough, our desire to change this pattern will become greater than our fear of letting it go. And that's when the pattern will drop.

Until then, let's not kid ourselves. No matter who shows up as the knight in shining armor, it's really the bogeyman. He is the abuser we hired when we made the choice to do something we really didn't want to do.

Alas, it's time to pick up the pieces, because Humpty Dumpty has come off the wall again. However, we don't have to put him back in the same precarious position.

KARMA

Alandro: Your books are truly remarkable. You have dived deeply into your own heart and have discovered the treasures that lie there and have enabled many of us to recognize those same treasures in ourselves. Thank you for your service.

I struggle with the notion of karma. I am Buddhist. The Buddha said that if you try to get your head around the concept of karma, you will go crazy. He seemed to suggest that it was important to accept its mystery. I know what he meant!

The popular New Age notion that you create your own reality does not sit well with me. I cannot believe that every event or person that spirals into our lives is somehow causally related to some aspect within ourselves. If I am angry, I will continually meet angry people. Or, if I am generous enough with others, I might attract a new Camaro into my life! In other words, the appearance of externals in my life is connected to my inner state.

To what extent do you believe this is true? In Buddhism, the focus is more on the effect of one's actions on one's inner state. Karma is more about the mental conditions, skillful or not, that we cultivate and that affect our lives. There is no emphasis on how the inner world will determine outer events in any predictable way. I am more comfortable with this notion. Yet, I am intrigued by the relationship between inner and outer at the same time.

When people and events come into our lives, how should we best interpret them—as reflections of our inner world or as simple random occurrences? Any insight you have would be appreciated.

Paul: The reason Buddha said that you would go crazy if you try to grasp this mentally is that you are trying to squeeze the ocean into your tea cup. It's not that it won't work . . . it's just that you might have a little collateral damage!

It is not possible to grasp non-linear concepts with the linear mind. Why keep trying?

With that caveat, I will say the following. The linear mind creates duality. It says either/or: either external situations are caused by our internal states or they are not. The non-linear, intuitive mind knows that either/or is really both/and.

Internal states obviously have an impact on external situations and external situations have an impact on internal states. What happens outside and what happens inside are connected by our actions, not in a straight line, but in a circular way. You know the expression "What comes around goes around?" That is a simple observation that we tend to give back what we receive and receive what we give.

To get off the wheel of Karma, we must make a rare and courageous choice: to love our enemies. Now that does not mean that our enemies will choose to love us. It just means that we offer them an opportunity to choose love. Whether they do or not is up to them.

Of course, you don't necessarily get a new Camaro just because you love your enemies. That's the linear mind trying to take charge. Buddha realized he'd never know about that Camaro, so he just gave up the desire to find the formula to it all. He knew that getting off the wheel of Karma did not at all depend on intellectually figuring out the specifics of how Karma worked.

He started with a far more simple proposition: to end suffering, drop your expectations. Cultivate detachment. Be with what happens and forget about what *you want* to happen. That's spiritual practice. If you practice, you learn how to be with what is, moment to moment. You drop your own internal drama—your reactions to what happens—and that makes it easier for you to be present for life as it unfolds. The result is greater peace within.

Does greater peace in your heart/mind lead to greater peace in your life? I will let you answer that question. And if you can't, don't worry about it. Just practice releasing your expectations and you will find out.

When you find out, will you let out a belly laugh? Hysterical tears? Or maybe nothing at all? Will there be a mountain or no mountain? Will you even be there?

What is the meaning of life? Of death? Is there any time in this embodiment or any embodiment in which all this gets explained to us? Can we find the chapter we're now living in the celestial user's manual and would it make any difference if we could?

You see, the questions go on forever. If you want my advice, just drink your tea and leave the ocean for swimming in... Anyway, arguing with Buddha is even less effective than arguing with Jesus!

HOW DO YOU LIKE THEM APPLES?

Carla: I am slowly reading your book with complete awe. My father and I were discussing the three important ingredients to faith: believing that God can do anything, believing that He will, and believing that He already has! I can only feel the first one.

I have had so many bad things happen to me in my life that I am unable to trust—especially GOD! Where is He now that my husband left me and our three kids? I want to attain the enlightenment that people like you have. Please help!

Paul: I wonder if, when you were a child, your father read you *The Little Engine that Could?* Like the little engine, you won't be able to accomplish much in life, if you don't believe that you can. We want to put everything in God's lap, but I must tell you there is no lap to put things in if you do not believe in yourself.

If you aren't willing to do something, God won't be able to

help you. Your willingness is the absolute core issue.

Now there are two ways that you can interfere with the spontaneous flow of abundance and grace in your life.

1. Think you can control what happens. Sorry, that isn't possible.

2. Think you are powerless to do anything. That too is an illusion.

Of course, if you are a control addict (#1), an ability to surrender and let go (#2) serves as a kind of antidote. On the other hand, if you believe that you are powerless, a little empowerment belief (#1) might help balance things out. However, the idea is to get away from these extremes.

You do this by tuning into what you want. Forget about what you think you want or what you think others might want from you. What is true in your belly? Where are you willing to invest your energy? What are you willing to enthusiastically commit to?

Until you can answer those questions, leave God out of the picture. And everyone else for that matter, including your ex-husband!

When you know what you want, start asking for it. Don't demand it or beat people up with your expectations. Just ask for it directly. Tell people what you want. Do it, of course, in a polite, respectful way without putting pressure on anyone. And then give people the freedom and the space to respond to you honestly.

If you ask for an apple, and an apple comes back, it doesn't mean that you are God's favorite child. It just means that it's apple season. Be happy. Celebrate your good fortune. Go ahead and eat that apple with great zest and commitment.

If you ask for an apple, and you get a banana, you can have two attitudes. One is: "At least it's a fruit!" The other is: "God doesn't like me because he sent me a banana and I hate bananas."

If you want something bad enough, getting a banana won't stop you. I learned that from an old and very wise monkey!

But most humans don't know that. Nine out of ten throw the banana back and then slip on the banana peel!

Remember, if it's banana season and you need an apple, you might have to be patient and wait for apple season! Are you willing to wait? How much do you really want an apple?

You see, this is completely about you. It has nothing to do with anyone else!

I can tell you that if you know what you want, if you are unwilling to accept substitutes, and if you are willing to be patient until what you want becomes available, you have a very good chance of succeeding. No, I can't give you a guarantee. Nobody can. Not even God. But I knew a guy once (actually it's a story in the Old Testament) who loved a girl and he was willing to work for seven years to gain her father's permission to marry her. And when he had finished working for that seven year period, he was told he had to work another seven years. So what did he do? He didn't throw up his hands in despair and walk away. He went back to work. And when he completed seven more years of hard labor, he was told he had to serve still another seven years—21 years in all. But he was not to be denied. Do you think God would oppose such a person?

You see, God is not really against us, but sometimes He decides to test our resolve.

Is there something that you want with your whole heart? If so, chances are, it will come to you. But it might not come to you when you want it and in the package you expect it to come in!

That's why the first question is: are you committed? And the second question is: are you patient and flexible?

If you are not committed and/or you are not patient and flexible, you probably won't be able to bring what you want into manifestation. Of course, I'm not saying that it's impossible. I'm just saying that the odds are against you.

So, you see, we are still talking about what you bring to the table and how you bring it. We aren't talking about God yet or about your ex-husband.

The truth is if you come to the table with flexibility and patience, it is only a matter of time before your heart's desire is fulfilled. Indeed, there is only one thing that can stand in the way of that fulfillment: your attitude. Think that you can't do it, and you won't do it. Think that it can happen only if it is done exactly as you think it should be done, and it won't happen.

Nothing happens without your cooperation! But nothing happens by force either.

You have heard the phrase "ready, willing, and able." Are you ready, willing and able? If so, be patient and the obstacles that block your way will gradually be removed.

When you realize that 90% of this story is about you, you'll take God, the ex-husband and me off the hook.

After all, I don't have something that you don't have. As I say in my book *Enlightenment for Everyone*, enlightenment is the realization of the light that is already within each one of us. It is in you as much as it is in me, and as much as it is in Jesus. That is His teaching. Let us not forget it.

TELLING THE TRUTH TO OURSELVES

Daniella: I just started to read your book *Love Without Conditions* and I would like a clarification from you when you say on page 28: *Bring your awareness to every thought and every feeling and you will soon find the source of your guilt and your subsequent suffering.* I am at present feeling angry at my siblings since we celebrated my sister's 50th birthday. This was organized by my siblings. I had my 50th birthday two years ago and no effort was made by anyone in the family to do anything special to celebrate it. I feel I have been a good and caring sister and have "been there for them" through thick and thin. I feel unappreciated and ignored by this. If I am guilty in this situation, I do not see it.

I would like to overcome my negative feeling and, instead of the blame, I would like to take responsibility for my feelings. I would appreciate a helping hand from you in clarifying how I should go about doing this.

Paul: As you will note, this section of the book suggests that the essence of forgiveness is self-forgiveness, not obtaining the forgiveness of others. We are the ones who establish our guilt and therefore we are the ones who must undo that guilt. We can do that only by taking the focus off what others do or do not do, and focusing instead on our own thoughts and feelings.

I suggest you focus on the following feeling you articulated in your letter: "I am at present feeling angry at my siblings." Please ask yourself where this anger originates? Does it come from a judgment you are making about them (that they do not value you as much as they value your sister)? What is the history of this judgment? Is it a brand new one, or one that you've had for many years?

Is it possible that you judge yourself as unworthy and their behavior toward you simply confirms your own belief about yourself? If so, your anger toward them may simply be a disguise for the anger you feel toward yourself. And in this case, whom do you need to forgive?

Is it possible that "not feeling important" is your belief about yourself and when someone triggers that belief you get angry at them, even though they may not actually feel that way about you? Be honest. Get to the root of your anger.

Have you communicated your anger to your siblings? If not, why not?

Remember, it is possible to communicate anger and still take responsibility for it. For example, you can say: "I feel angry because you celebrated our sister, and I did not think you celebrated me." You can ever go deeper: "Behind this anger, there is hurt. I feel hurt because it seems to me that you do not appreciate me as much as you appreciate our sister."

Remember: your conclusion may or may not be true. You don't know. You have to ask them to find out. Do you want to find out? Do you have the courage to tell the truth about how you feel and allow them to see the interpretation you are making of their behavior?

Sharing all this gets it out on the table, where all sides of the situation can be known.

However, when you say "I would like to overcome my negative feeling" I must stop you. Your job is not to try to overcome your negative feelings. That would be dishonest to yourself and to others. You must be with what you feel, not with what you "wish you felt."

Don't try to overcome your feelings. Just recognize them. Share them as honestly as you can without blaming anyone else. Let your anger and your hurt be known. Don't hide these feelings.

Express the feelings so that you can get to the truth, not so you can avoid it. Blaming others takes the focus off you and puts it onto someone else. It is avoidance.

Face what you feel honestly. Don't be ashamed. Your shame makes you want to make someone else responsible for how you are feeling. That is trespass.

Don't trespass. Just be authentic and tell the truth.

Accept that you feel "unappreciated and ignored." That is your truth. It may not be the ultimate truth of the situation, but it is your truth right now.

If you are ashamed of how you feel, own that shame or embarrassment. Acknowledge to yourself or others: I am judging myself because I feel "unappreciated and ignored." I think that a "spiritual" person shouldn't feel that way.

"I'm feeling like a bad girl: bad because I wasn't acknowledged on my birthday (so there must be something wrong with me!), bad because I need this attention, and bad because I'm angry that I didn't get it. I'm feeling bad, bad, bad, bad, bad . . . "

You get my drift.

Now, even if you do this process alone, you will have the opportunity to accept how you feel, forgive yourself for making all those judgments about others and about yourself, and reassure yourself that you are okay just as you are, judgments and all.

When you can forgive yourself like this, you don't need to go to others and ask them to change. You can bring the change in your own heart-mind.

The keys to the Kingdom are in your hands, Daniella. They will always be in your hands.

By all means tell others the truth. It helps to clear the air and bring honesty and healing for all parties. But most of all, tell yourself the truth.

MAKING A REAL LIVING

Klaus: Your books touch my heart very deeply. In the last chapter of *Return to the Garden* (which I read in the German translation) you talk about earning a living and giving your talents to the world. Right now I'm in a situation where I find it difficult to get a job and earn my living. I really feel discriminated against and banned out of the garden. Can you tell me how to deal with this in a constructive way?

Paul: First, you need to be clear about what your strengths are and what gives you the most joy (finding your gift). Then, you need to begin to move in this direction (trusting it).

The more you trust in your gift and give it without strings attached, the more it multiplies (that's what Jesus did with the loaves and fishes). The supply is always there. That is a condition of the Garden itself. It is ever abundant.

However, we don't trust the gift and we place conditions on giving and receiving it, so we reduce the supply available to us. Conversely, an open mind and heart never lack for good work, because they are willing to do whatever needs to be done and they do it joyfully

If you are feeling discriminated against, then you are probably looking outward for the Source of your gift, rather than inward, which is the direction from which it comes. If you are waiting for the validation/approval of others, you will wait a very long time. You must find that validation within yourself.

Once you validate yourself, giving your gift becomes easy because it is a fulfillment of who you are. You love to give your gift and you are delighted whenever it is received by anyone.

Another tip: the only real gift is the gift of love and acceptance. Give it to yourself. Give it to others. It is a REAL LIVING.

THE PERFECT STORM

Bertha: I need your help in understanding and changing my current situation. I have read several of your books and they have helped me make some positive changes in my life. For example, I began meditating regularly and practicing non-judgment. Because I maintained focus on myself and practiced unconditional love, my husband and I stopped arguing. Before this, we argued on a regular basis.

I truly felt peace and love in my life on a daily basis.

Then, a couple of years ago we found out we were pregnant, purchased a home, and I buried my sister who died of breast cancer. At that time, I became engaged in true co-dependent behavior in trying to help my siblings who seemed to be in much worse condition then myself. The change in me was almost instantaneous. I became nervous, anxious, and arguments with my husband began again, even worse then before.

I stopped meditating. I would pick up your book committed to reading it, but after reading a paragraph I'd put it down. I drowned myself in fear and had to stop working. My husband took over the finances, due to my high-risk pregnancy, and mismanaged our finances. This changed our economic status and the lifestyle I was used to shifted dramatically.

I know that I am living the consequences of my choices. I just don't know how to move on. I am literally stuck. When I make a mental commitment to change, I break my commitment within 24 hours. How do I get my heart into it? I feel so much pain because I know what I could be living if only I would change.

My heart feels like it's broken. I have much less time now that I am a mother and currently expecting our second child. Please help me get unstuck.

Paul: You can't force yourself to do something that you don't want to do. Please don't try. Instead, honor the fact that you are not ready to do this.

You say that your heart feels broken. Have you taken the time you need to feel your pain and mourn your losses? Have you taken the time to feel and express your anger?

Your heart is asking you for some attention. Please give this attention to your emotional body. How can you give others love if you don't find time to love yourself?

It's great to feel peaceful, but life is not always peaceful. Sometimes difficult and challenging things happen and we need to get our arms around our entire experience. That means taking the time to courageously feel everything that we feel. Denying our feelings will not lead to peace.

Be glad that you have not been able to use meditation as a tool for denial. Be glad that you have been unable "to pretend" that you are happy when you are not happy. Congratulations for reaching out and asking for help in the midst of your discomfort.

Please don't try to get rid of these feelings. They are there for a reason. They are a pathway to the heart.

It's easy to read books and live our spirituality on the intellectual level . . . easy, that is, until life comes in and clobbers us. Then we are forced to go deeper in our spirituality.

The door to your heart wants to open now. Will you have the courage to open it?

Meditation is fine, but I would heartily recommend *Affinity Group* practice to you. Meeting once a week with a group of people who hold the space for honest, heartfelt communion will provide you with the support you need to accept your feelings and work with them, instead of against them.

Do you think you are the only one being clobbered? I assure you that you are not! Participating in an *Affinity Group* will drive that point home to you every week.

In addition to *Affinity Group* practice, I suggest a daily practice of going into the silence for fifteen minutes two to three times per day. During this time just witness your thoughts and be aware of your feelings. Focus on your heart and bring your breath into your abdomen. Ask yourself. "How am I doing right now? Am I loving myself? Am I finding fault with myself? What's going on with me right now in this moment?"

This practice will slow things down a little so that you can begin to be with your experience, accept whatever is happening, including your judgments, and hold it all compassionately. My book *Enlightenment for Everyone* has a number of related practices that you may find helpful.

You will find information about *Affinity Groups* on my website (www.paulferrini.com). If there isn't a group in your area, I encourage you to start one. It's time to give your heart the nurturing it needs.

If you ignore the warning signs, the downward spiral will probably continue. Don't wait for the next big storm, grab the life raft now and paddle for shore.

CLAIRVOYANCE AND SEEING CLEARLY

Tyler: I am 18 years old. About a year and a half ago I started seeing angels and auras, only I didn't understand what they were. I went in search of an answer and found a healer I trusted. He told me that I am clairvoyant.

I have since begun to see much more and to hear voices and to talk with souls who are not from most people's world. I go and talk to a lady named Margaret and she is a real help to me. She calls me a star child.

My question is this: I don't like what I see and know. I think of it more as a curse, although the people around me seem to think of it as a gift. I find it very hard to tell anyone about this and I don't know how to relate to the people around me anymore. I very rarely do anything about what I see and it is never spoken of in my home with my parents. They aren't like me at all.

Do you think that God is going to be angry with me because

of how I feel? I really know very little about the spiritual world. I don't want to harm anyone. I never asked for this.

Paul: You say "I go and talk to a lady named Margaret, and she is a real help to me." If she is a real help to you, then this is a positive activity and it doesn't hurt you or anyone else. If it ceases to be a help, you can stop going.

However, you also say "I don't like what I see and know. I think of it more as a curse than a gift." How you feel about your experience is what is most important. Seeing it as a curse cannot possibly help you accept your abilities and use them for your good and that of others.

I suggest that you spend some time each morning when you get up and each evening before you go to bed in prayer. Ask that you see only what can be truly helpful to yourself and others. Repeat that prayer any time during the day when you see something you don't like.

Also, please remember that only love is real. Everything else is simply some form of lack of love. Only love brings peace and healing, so stay centered in your love for yourself and others.

Remember, if you feel fear, you are not aligned with love. You are giving your power away to what you see. Close your eyes and turn within to the source of love. Feel God's unconditional love for you and for others. Then what you see can be seen through the eyes of that love.

And finally "Do you think that God is going to be angry with me because of how I feel?" No, God is not angry at you. God wants only that you receive His love and share it with others.

Of course, not everything that you see will be helpful or loving, so you need to discriminate. Use what is helpful and throw the rest away. Separate the wheat from the chaff. This is a spiritual practice.

Just as there are physical voices that you would do well not to listen to, because what they say is not helpful to you or anyone else, so there are non-physical voices you should not listen to for the same reason.

So, as you see, the question is not whether the gift is a blessing or a curse. The question is how will you use it? Your intention will determine whether this ability you have brings help or hurt.

In Corinthians it is said: "First they saw through a glass darkly and then face to face." To see "face to face" is to see things as they are without distortion, without interpretation. That is what true clairvoyance is.

Just because one sees things not of this world does not mean that one sees them truly, clearly, or as they are. Seeing clearly is a discipline.

When you can see without prejudice, predisposition or fear, then the lens will be clear. Until then, you or anyone else will be seeing through a dark or cloudy lens.

Please don't complain about the lens. Just take care of it: clean it regularly. Then, there will be the least possibility for distortion.

Clairvoyance can be a curse only for those who do not accept the discipline of spiritual practice (for those who don't clean the lens on a regular basis). And by "discipline of spiritual practice" I mean the moment by moment, day by day alignment with love.

Love is the only cleaning fluid that works. We must be baptized in the waters of love not just once, but every day of our lives if we want to see clearly. For without love there is no truth, but only opinion. And all opinion injures someone. All interpretation is a form of trespass.

When we see "what is," the mask is lifted. That is when we see face to face. That is when we see each other as God sees us.

LOVE, ADDICTION AND SELF-BETRAYAL

Alida: I read two of your books in the German translation one year ago and I was wondering if you can help me with a difficult situation.

For ten months I have been in love with a man who lives 220 kilometers from me. I recently found out that he gets drunk a lot, "chats" with people on the internet and watches porno films. He started lying to me about all these things and I told him that I could not live with those lies anymore and that I was going to leave him.

He told me that he loved me but was unconsciously doing these things, not realizing that they hurt me. After that I was willing to stay with him.

I think that we really love each other deeply. In fact, I think, I never loved before I met him. And I am 30 years old.

We are now planning to move in together, but he must decide if he is willing to give up his secure job and move to my place.

I am wondering if he is going to keep drinking when we live together. Should I even be taking the risk to live together with an alcohol sick man? I was bulimic for 13 years, so I know what addiction means.

Paul: It is wonderful to love. Love lifts us up. It inspires us. It enables us to feel a level of intimacy and connection that takes us beyond our selfish, egotistical perspective. So what I say to you I am saying in this context. Love can be the greatest blessing.

However, even the greatest blessing can be turned into a curse if we try to control each other. Each one of us must be free to give as we are able to give or our gift is meaningless.

I congratulate you on setting limits. You have the right to say that you don't want to be around someone who drinks and watches porno films. You have a right to stand up for yourself and ask for what you want. This is important. If you don't do this, you will betray yourself.

However, you have no right to ask anyone else to change for your sake. If your friend wants to stop drinking and watching pornography, then he will take responsibility for doing this on his own. He will change because he wants to, not because you want him to.

Moving in with him before he has accomplished what you require is tantamount to asking for serious trouble. If you really love each other, go slowly with this. Do not pressure him to move. Moving will likely put more pressure on him and increase his instability.

Instead, encourage him to stabilize on his own where he is (or, if he really wants to move, help him to find his own place and job and get settled in the city where you reside). Allow him the time and space to stop drinking and develop a lifestyle he is proud of . . . because he wants to feel good about himself, not because you want him to do these things.

Love him as he is and allow him to be himself. Give him this freedom or you will risk losing your own.

There is nothing more difficult than trying to redeem another human being. It's like trying to rescue a drowning person with one arm tied behind your back. Those who try either get pulled down and drown themselves, or they return empty-handed and feel guilty for failing to fulfill a responsibility that never truly belonged to them.

So, Alida, give your friend the freedom to decide what he wants. Take off all the pressure. Give him space and love him from a distance.

See if he moves toward you or away from you. Take the time to find out if this relationship truly supports both of you in being yourselves or whether it is an invitation to mutual self-betrayal.

Be patient. It is a lot harder to undo a co-dependent relationship than it is to get into one.

Please allow for the possibility that your friend drinks and watches porno films because he wants to. If so, any attempt to prevent him from doing these things trespasses on him and violates his freedom to choose his own life.

Don't do that. Nothing good can come of it.

To put it in a nutshell: we all want to be loved, but when we give ourselves up or try to take another hostage for the sake of that love, we overburden that love from the start.

It is ironic. Love promises the possibility of release from ego-consciousness, yet as soon as we love someone our ego goes crazy and tries to take control.

That is the nature of our experience. We just need to be aware of it and keep surrendering to love without conditions.

WORKING WITH DEPRESSION

Guiseppi: I have just recovered from another eight days of depression. It is a cycle I have been dealing with for over thirty years now.

In 1979, I started to search beyond medical advice for depression and look for my own answers. This exploration took me into a five year study of the effects foods and chemical pollutants had on my mind and eventually to the awareness of the spiritual element of my existence.

I discovered *A Course in Miracles* in 1988 and I have been working with this material in the hope that it will assist me in becoming free from depression.

In the past two years, I have witnessed that my depressions are being caused by my choice not to love on some level. Indeed, I have on occasion experienced my depressions lifting within minutes after recognizing my unloving thoughts and offering blessings instead. This is miraculous considering my history of depressions lasting for weeks or even a whole year.

This last depression of eight days eventually dissipated by my effort of constantly ignoring my fear thoughts and keeping my trust and attention on the tiniest feeling of love that I am capable of being aware of.

Past advice from spiritual teachers has been "let your fears have you." I have tried just being with my fears, consciously for hours at a time, but they are never ending. My fears in depression are that the world is empty and meaningless and there is no point in living.

I believe I am at the stage the *Course* talks about when I

realize that the world as I am seeing it "is" meaningless. Most of the time, I am at peace with this knowledge because I am trusting that Spirit is guiding me to see the world through loving eyes. However, on an unconscious level, my fear of a meaningless world from time to time overwhelms me in the form of depression.

My current answer to this is to be aware that my fears are my ego trying to fill the void and that my task is to be gentle with myself despite the fear and keep my attention on the tiny feeling of love.

What I am asking is "is there any way I could say no to my depressions and they would be gone?'

Currently, I wake up some mornings and the threat of emptiness and isolation is particularly strong. I try to ignore it by focusing exclusively on love for as long as it takes for the fear to go (sometimes hours); I have to be patient and try to be calm and wait it out. This last time was eight days of hell to me.

I do my breathing of course and this has broken my depressions long before I read your guidance. But I have found no magic wand except persistent trust in love. At the same time, it is small consolation to know I am not just doing this for me but for everyone.

Paul: Yes, we all need to learn to hold ourselves and our fears in a loving and compassionate way, but no, you are not doing it for anyone else. You are doing it for you.

The question seems to be what to do when the fear and sense of meaningless comes up. You would like to ignore it or push it away and instead focus on love. And this, my dear brother, is not a loving act. The means and the goal are not congruent, a common byproduct of Miraclespeak.

Love is simply not compatible with resistance or denial. Trying to make the fear go away, trying to ignore it, or shift it is not embracing our experience. Embracing the fear means acknowledging it and being with it without judgment. Or, in simple terms, it means "letting it be okay that you are afraid."

Can you see that you are innocent even though you are afraid? Can you feel the fear and know that you are okay and that God does not love you any less because you are afraid? Can you feel your vulnerability, your pain, your suffering without judging it?

You see: this is spiritual practice. It is hard to read your letter without having a fairly direct and clear sense that your so called "depression" is the instrument of your spiritual work. It drives you to understand and to have compassion for yourself. And as that compassion for yourself grows, it expands to include others. So it is a great work of the heart.

Upon hearing about a couple of people who were struggling with their relationship, Bill Thetford (co-creator of the *Course*) was purported to have said: "Let the bastards come in so that we can forgive them!" At least Bill had a sense of humor.

We all need to have a sense of humor.

To be sure, there comes a time when the things that used to give meaning to our lives no longer do so. Indeed, there are many times like this. We attach and detach, ebb and flow. That is the nature of our existence.

Yet the background behind the coming and the going is a steady hum, a neutral color against which all the other colors read out. Call it what you will, this indivisible oneness is always with us. It accepts us when we cannot accept ourselves. And it sings us when we have no voice for singing.

It is singing you right now.

Somewhere I hear a man crying because he is sad, and laughing because everything he ever believed in has been stripped away from him. He is not ashamed. Indeed, for the first time in his life, he feels truly free.

That man is you, brother.

Guiseppi: The morning after I read your answer to my question, I woke to another encounter with "is this all there is?" depression which I tried to stem by focusing on the feeling of love. All day I did my best to do this, but by bed time I had sunk into a full blown depression.

The next morning I wrote out your answer in my diary and had the following awareness:

I'm beginning to accept and have compassion for the me that is frightened. I recognize that pushing this me to love is not loving and understanding.

The goal of love is very frightening to the fearful me. I have long recognized this, but recognition is not enough. Gentle, tender, loving care and compassion is what the frightened me wants. Not the push of my (late) father in me.

This deeper understanding and acceptance immediately reduced the fear and tension and by the end of the day the depression had dissolved. Thank you for your help and insight.

WITH OUR WHOLE HEART

Jerome: I would like to ask about decision making, responsibility, and divine guidance. I am currently about to choose my university courses for the fall term, except I don't want to return to school.

I am afraid that I won't be able to bring a sense of peace and centeredness into the world of academia. Also, I feel like I would enjoy doing something less intellectual with my time.

I have borrowed a lot of money so far to attend school and it seems like it would be in my best material interest to continue and get a degree. I find it difficult to locate my SELF in all the conflicting desires.

My question is how do I bring peace and guidance into my decision making? I don't want to be controlled by my fears, or by the fears of others (social expectations). How do I find my SELF underneath the burden of responsibility I feel?

Paul: It is impossible to read your letter without seeing that you don't want to be in school. My first question to you is therefore a simple one: are you going to do what you want to do or are you going to do what you think you "should" do?

Then, if you decide to do what you want to do, are you going to do it full force with no regrets or are you going to keep wondering if you "should" have stayed in school?

Or if you decide to stay in school, are you going to give it your very best effort, even if it's hard for you, or are you going to put off your work and sit around fantasizing about how it "could" have been if you had left school?

You see, if you make either choice wholeheartedly and do the very best you can, then you won't experience so much conflict.

If you can't make either choice wholeheartedly, the best thing that you can do is embrace your ambivalence and stop putting pressure on yourself to decide. Perhaps you could take a semester off and practice being patient with yourself and accepting all of the voices within your psyche.

You don't have to act on any of these voices. Just listen to them and hear what they need to say to you.

If you make your ambivalence okay, it will move when it is ready to move. Direction will come when it's time.

We can't force ourselves to choose before we are ready. If we do, we will probably have regrets.

As you know, the greatness that you seek is within you. It does not exist in the world.

The real question is not whether you go to school or not, but how can you best honor yourself, doubts and all?

I leave you with that question. It is obviously not up to me to answer it for you.

Author's Postscript

THE NEED FOR DIALOGUE

In reading through these pages, I am struck most of all by the need that all of us have for spiritual conversation. We are trying as best we can to understand spiritual law and come into alignment with it.

I recall how people were drawn to Martin Buber to talk about the meaning of life. And I remember how Sean and I used to meet at the old Coffee Connection in Harvard Square in Cambridge to discuss spiritual books and to look at what was happening in our lives from a spiritual perspective.

We don't live in a time when going to church or temple fulfills this need. There is no Rabbi I can discuss Torah with, except perhaps the one whose teachings permeate these pages. And of course, had I not been in great pain, had I not called out for that conversation, none of this would have come to be.

Jesus is one of my teachers, and Martin Buber, Lao Tzu, Rumi are others. They are part of a community of people who speak a language that I can understand. Perhaps that is because they have suffered as I have suffered, because they have asked the same questions I have asked.

My teachers come from many traditions, but every one of them hears the call of my heart. They don't always have the answers I need, but they know my questions. They know the all-consuming fire of the inquiry, the search for meaning, the loneliness of the journey and the joy of insight and understanding.

They are not afraid to sit with me when I am in pain, or to dance with me when I feel joy. They are not afraid of my doubt, my fear or my unhappiness. They are not embarrassed by my love for them or my bliss.

I don't have to be morally good, spiritually correct, or socially appropriate to deserve their company. I have only to be who I am, to feel what I feel. It is that fellowship, that intimacy that links me to them.

Over the years in which the Christ Mind material has been written, it has become clear to me that others have been touched by this teaching in much the same way that I was. Many people have told me that reading my words has made a deep impression on them. Some have told me that it has saved their lives.

I feel grateful to be a mouthpiece for a teaching that ministers to the deepest places in our hearts, a teaching that refuses to be intimidated by our pain or our fear, and helps us learn how to love when we think love is impossible. Were it not for this teaching—and the great ones who brought it to me—I too would have been a casualty of my own fearful drama. How could I do anything else but offer the same life raft to others shipwrecked on the overwhelming seas of blame and shame. I know that as you embrace the truth within your own heart, you too will be called to trust the inner wisdom and offer to others the essence of this teaching in your own unique way.

BREAKING BREAD TOGETHER

Each of us must give back so that the next generation may find its way. We are like Hansel and Gretel dropping crumbs in the woods, so that the way home will not disappear even though we have an imminent encounter with the wicked witch.

We can't avoid that encounter, nor can those who come after us, but we can mark the way back home.

No one escapes the pain and sorrow of life. But not all find meaning in it. To find meaning you must not be afraid to ask "why?" even though no one around you seems to have the answer. And you must have the courage to keep asking, even when the answers you once had prove to be painfully inadequate.

Unless we ask the great questions (Why am I here? Why do I suffer? Why do I have to die?), we will get lost in the drama of our lives without having any idea what, if anything, is being asked of us here.

Asking the great questions is what happens when we gather in spiritual community. For some of us, spiritual community may not be found in our home town. Those who share our questions and our search for meaning live all over the globe. Yet, our communion is no less important than if they lived next door.

To be in community means to be in dialog with others about the great questions. Martin Buber understood this and his door was always open to those who wished to be in dialog with him. I imagine that some of those discussions were quite lively. Others I suspect took place in silence.

If you are reading these words, then the possibility for dialog continues. And it does not end with us.

We are part of an unbroken tradition of people asking the great questions. To be sure, we don't have the same answer to these questions. Indeed, we often squabble about who has the best answer. But, in our hearts we know that there is not, nor can there ever be, one answer for everyone.

We may believe in One God, but we will never agree on what that God looks like. Indeed, in our tradition, it is said that God is really indescribable. And that the very attempt to describe God distances us from Him or Her.

In our tradition, being close to God has a lot to do with asking questions and not with having answers. It has a lot to do with living in the mystery.

In fact, it just may be that the need to know God simply is not compatible with the desire to experience God. And perhaps that is why those who have experienced the mystery of the divine come away speechless.

Not withstanding the futility of approaching God with the intellect, we still crave discussion and dialog. I think that is because conversation makes us feel less isolated and alone. Being alone with the big questions is scary, especially since these questions not are asked in an abstract fashion, but rise up from the emotional fabric of our lives. The pain of separation and loss are as much as part of our lives as the joy of sharing and intimacy. It helps to be able to connect with others on both ends of the emotional spectrum.

True spiritual community is not about having the answers for ourselves or for others. It is about sharing our experience and listening to the experience of others. It is about giving and receiving compassion and comfort. It is about fellowship and family.

We are all members of one great family. One day we will realize that there is no one who is excluded from that family and welcome all to break bread with us. That is what the master meant when he said "take this bread, it is my body." The bread we share together is spiritual food and sustenance. And the wine we sip is the fruit of the emotional body—the sharing of our joy and our pain. Is it any wonder that we drink from the same cup and break from the same loaf.

I welcome all of you to the table. May you drink deeply and chew slowly. May you offer this bread and wine to others, as it has been offered to you. I send you my love and my blessings.

Paul Ferrini

Appendix

Clearly, in the aftermath of the recent terrorist attacks on New York City and Washington, there is no better time to be looking for love in the depths of our hearts and souls. It is not easy to connect with love when we are hurt and afraid. But we have no choice if we want to heal and move on.

Toward that end, I have included here a poem that I wrote on the National Day of Mourning for the victims of these attacks. This poem celebrates the unselfish actions of many of our citizens and calls the people of our country to our highest and best response.

The Root of Love:

Notes for a National Day of Mourning: September 14, 2001

I am proud of my country
because at a time when thousands of people
have been brutally executed
by a few heartless men,
the tears in our president's eyes
speaker louder than his vows of retribution,

because, at a time when you could expect
the voices of hatred and vengeance
to be loudest in the land,
it is the voices of caring and compassion
that resonate like hundreds of chimes
moving in the wind:

men digging for brothers in the rubble,
families of victims comforting other families,
volunteers from all walks of life—
doctors, nurses, firemen, policemen,
people of all races and religions
coming together as one family.

I am proud of my country
because it stood undefended and trusting at the edge of land
where the lady of sorrows holds her flame,
welcoming strangers to a place
where differences in ideas and backgrounds
are not only tolerated,
but integrated into the fabric of our lives,
making us all stronger.

I am proud of my country
because its borders have always been open
to those from other lands
who are mistreated or oppressed,
because we hold the hope of freedom and justice
not just for ourselves
but for all the peoples of the world.

I am proud of my country
not because we are perfect (we aren't)
nor because we always practice what we preach (we don't),
but because we aspire to be fair, generous and kind,
and because, no matter how difficult or embarrassing it is,
we try to acknowledge our mistakes
and learn from them.

Like most countries, we have a dark side too.
That's why we are learning to apologize
to our black brothers and sisters
for years of slavery and abuse,
and to our Japanese citizens for sending their families
into internment camps during World War II.

There are very few Americans who do not feel in their hearts
the pain of Hiroshima or My Lai.
Most of us are not proud of our mistakes.
Most of us do not dance in the streets
when we see the pain and suffering of other people.

Today is a day to mourn the deaths of our citizens
and to send our prayers to their families and friends.
It is a day to be righteous in our anger
and stalwart in our resolve to see justice done.
But it is also a day to remember who we are
and who we are not.

We are not the people these terrorists take us for.
Even those who celebrated this act of brutality
in the streets of Jerusalem
can see if they look:
We are a nation of people who love each other.

We don't have one religion or one color of skin.
We don't have one economic or political idea.
Our differences are monumental,
but so is our capacity to bridge those differences
and come together when our freedom is threatened.

Those who don't know this about us
will learn of it now.
They will learn that we value not just our own freedom,
but theirs as well; not just our own lives,
but their lives too.

That is why we will act with equal measures
of courage and restraint.
We will not target innocent people
in other countries or in our own.
We will defend ourselves and, in so doing,
We will defend them too.

We are a nation of people who care about each other.
It is not just our military might and our material wealth
that define America.
It is our love, our trust, and our compassion.
It is our fairness and commitment to equality.
That is who we are.

And that is why those who attack us cannot prevail,
for to prevail against us would be to destroy
the very values that enable human beings
to live spiritual lives,
to live in a world where fear is stronger than love,
where freedom and trust are absent.

We do not want to live in such a world.
I don't think they do either.

I don't know a lot about Islam,
but I know this.
Muhammad was a man who loved God
and he loved all of us equally.

He would not condone killing for any reason.
Like Jesus, Moses, Buddha,
and the other great spiritual teachers of the planet,
he wanted us to respect our differences
and learn to live in peace together.

He knew that no war is holy and only madmen
call for death and destruction in God's name.
Hurting other people is not spiritual.
Not in Islam, in Christianity or in Judaism.
That I know.
And I think all of us know it.

What is spiritual is to find the Source of love
in the midst of our fear and our pain,
to learn to reach out to each other
when history and culture
threaten to divide us into two warring camps.

That isn't easy to do, but there is no other choice.
And in that respect, America will lead the way.

You can see it in the faces of our leaders,
our media people, and our citizens.

America is awake
and digging down deep
not just to bury its victims
but to draw strength
from the deepest place in our souls
where love is rooted.

Paul Ferrini

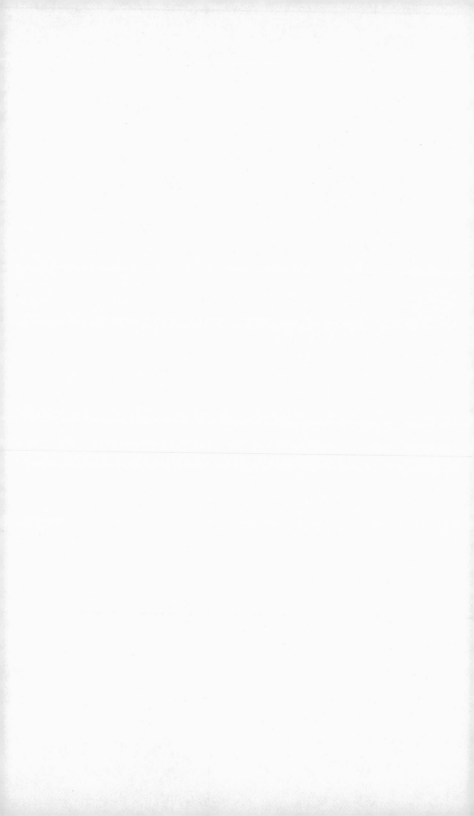

Paul Ferrini's unique blend of radical Christianity and other wisdom traditions, goes beyond self-help and recovery into the heart of healing. His conferences, retreats, and *Affinity Group Process* have helped thousands of people deepen their practice of forgiveness and open their hearts to the divine presence in themselves and others.

For more information on Paul's workshops and retreats or The *Affinity Group Process,* check out the web-site at *www.paulferrini.com,* email: heartway@crocker.com or write to Heartways Press, P. O. Box 99, Greenfield, MA 01302.

New Release from Heartways Press

Opening our Hearts to the Lessons of Love

DANCING *with the* BELOVED

Opening our hearts to the lessons of love
PAUL FERRINI

Dancing with the Beloved
by Paul Ferrini
ISBN 1-879159-47-3
160 pages paperback $12.95

Romance may open the door to love, but it does not help us walk through it. Something else is needed. Something deeper. Something ultimately more real.

Challenging times must be weathered. Love must be strengthened beyond neediness and self-interest. It must die a thousand deaths to learn to rise like the phoenix beyond adversity of any kind.

Love is not a fragile, shiny thing, kept separate from the pain and misery of life. It is born of our willingness to learn from our mistakes and encounter the depth of our pain, as well as our partner's pain. That is the way it is.

In time we learn that all pain is the same pain. And we have compassion for the other people who inadvertently step on our toes as they learn to find the inner rhythms of the dance. Like us, they will stumble and fall hundreds of times until that moment of profound acceptance when grace comes and the beloved takes their hand in the circle.

Books and Tapes
available from Heartways Press

Paul Ferrini's luminous new translation captures the essence of Lao Tzu and the fundamental aspects of Taoism in a way that no single book ever has!

The Great Way of All Beings:
Renderings of Lao Tzu
by Paul Ferrini
ISBN 1-879159-46-5
320 pages hardcover $23.00

The Great Way of All Beings: Renderings of Lao Tzu is composed of two different versions of Lao Tzu's masterful scripture *Tao Te Ching.* Part one, *River of Light,* is an intuitive, spontaneous rendering of the material that captures the spirit of the *Tao Te Ching,* but does not presume to be a close translation. Part Two is a more conservative translation of the *Tao Te Ching* that attempts as much as possible to stay with the words and images used in the original text. The words and images used in Part One leap out from the center to explore how the wisdom of the Tao touches us today. By contrast, the words and images of Part Two turn inward toward the center, offering a more feminine, receptive version of the material.

"We listen for it, yet its note can't be heard.
We look intently for it, yet its image can't be seen.

Although it has no beginning,
it leads us back to our original nature

Although it has no end,
it helps us come to completion."

A Practical Guide to Realizing your True Nature

"Enlightenment is the realization of the light that is within you. It is the conscious recognition and acceptance of that light. Enlightenment is discovering who you already are and being it fully."

Enlightenment for Everyone
by Paul Ferrini
with an Introduction by Iyanla Vanzant
ISBN 1-879159-45-7
160 pages hardcover $16.00

Enlightenment is not contingent on finding the right teacher or having some kind of peak spiritual experience. There's nothing that you need to get, find or acquire to be enlightened. You don't need a priest or rabbi to intercede with God for you. You don't need a special technique or meditation practice. You don't need to memorize scripture or engage in esoteric breathing practices. You simply need to discover who you already are and be it fully. This essential guide to self-realization contains eighteen spiritual practices that will enable you to awaken to the truth of your being. This exquisite hard-cover book will be a life-long companion and will make an inspirational gift to friends and family.

A comprehensive selection from the Christ Mind teachings published by Doubleday

"Open yourself now to the wisdom of Jesus, as Paul Ferrini has brought it through. These words can inspire you to greater insights and understandings, to more clarity and a grander resolve to make changes in your life that can truly change the world."

Neale Donald Walsch, author of *Conversations with God.*

Reflections of the Christ Mind: The Present Day Teachings of Jesus
by Paul Ferrini
Introduction by Neale Donald Walsch
ISBN 0-385-49952-3
302 pages hardcover $19.95

Reflections of the Christ Mind contains key excerpts from *Love Without Conditions, Silence of the Heart, Miracle of Love* and *Return to the Garden*. It presents the most important teachings in the *Christ Mind* series.

I am the Door
by Paul Ferrini
ISBN 1-879159-41-4
288 pages hardcover $21.95

Years ago, Paul Ferrini began hearing a persistent inner voice that said "I want you to acknowledge me." He also had a series of dreams in which Jesus appeared to teach him. Later, when Ferrini's relationship with his teacher was firmly established, the four books in the *Reflections of the Christ Mind* series were published. Here, in this lovely lyrical collection, we can hear the voice of Jesus speaking directly to us about practical topics of everyday life that are close to our hearts like work and livelihood, relationships, community, forgiveness, spiritual practices, and miracles. When you put this book down, there will no doubt in your mind that the teachings of the master are alive today. Your life will never be the same.

Taking Back Our Schools
by Paul Ferrini
ISBN 1-879159-43-0 $10.95

This book is written for parents who are concerned about the education of their children. It presents a simple idea that could transform the school system in this country. This book does not pretend to have all the answers. It is the start of a conversation. It is chapter one in a larger book that has not yet been written. If you choose to work with these ideas, you may be one of the authors of the chapters to come.

The Way of Peace
by Paul Ferrini
ISBN 1-879159-42-2
256 pages hardcover
$19.95

The Way of Peace is a simple method for con-necting with the wisdom and truth that lie within our hearts. The two hundred and sixteen oracular mes-sages in this book were culled from the bestselling *Reflections of the Christ Mind* series by Paul Ferrini.

Open this little book spontaneously to receive inspirational guidance, or ask a formal question and follow the simple div-inatory procedure described in the introduction. You will be amazed at the depth and the accuracy of the response you receive.

Like the *I-Ching*, the *Book of Runes,* and other systems of guid-ance, *The Way of Peace* empowers you to connect with peace within and act in harmony with your true self and the unique circumstances of your life.

Special dice, blessed by the author, are available for using *The Way of Peace* as an oracle. To order, send $3.00 plus shipping.

Grace Unfolding: The Art of Living A Surrendered Life
96 pages paperback $9.95
ISBN 1-879159-37-6

As we surrender to the truth of our being, we learn to relinquish the need to control our lives, figure things out, or predict the future. We begin to let go of our judgments and interpretations and accept life the way it is. When we can be fully present with whatever life brings, we are guided to take the next step on our journey. That is the way that grace unfolds in our lives.

"The Road to Nowhere is the path through your heart.
It is not a journey of escape. It is a journey through your pain
to end the pain of separation."

Illuminations on the Road to Nowhere
160 pages paperback $12.95
ISBN 1-879159-44-9

There comes a time for all of us when the outer destinations no longer satisfy and we finally understand that the love and happiness we seek cannot be found outside of us. It must be found in our own hearts, on the other side of our pain.

This book makes it clear that we can no longer rely on outer teachers or teachings to find our spiritual identity. Nor can we find who we are in relationships where boundaries are blurred and one person makes decisions for another. If we want to be authentic, we can't allow anyone else to be an authority for us, nor can we allow ourselves to be an authority for others.

This provocative book challenges many of our basic assumptions about personal happiness and the meaning of our relationship with others and with God.

The Relationship Book You've Been Waiting For

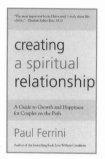

Creating a Spiritual Relationship: A Guide to Growth and Happiness for Couples on the Path

144 pages paperback $10.95

ISBN 1-879159-39-2

This simple but profound guide to growth and happiness for couples will help you and your partner:

• Make a realistic commitment to each other
• Develop a shared experience that nurtures your relationship
• Give each other the space to grow and express yourselves as individuals
• Communicate by listening without judgment and telling the truth in a non-blaming way
• Understand how you mirror each other
• Stop blaming your partner and take responsibility for your thoughts, feelings and actions
• Practice forgiveness together on an ongoing basis

These seven spiritual principles will help you weather the ups and downs of your relationship so that you and your partner can grow together and deepen the intimacy between you. The book also includes a special section on living alone and preparing to be in relationship and a section on separating with love when a relationship needs to change form or come to completion.

Return to the Garden
Reflections of The Christ Mind,
Part IV
$12.95, Paperback
ISBN 1-879159-35-X

"In the Garden, all our needs were provided for. We knew no struggle or hardship. We were God's beloved. But happiness was not enough for us. We wanted the freedom to live our own lives. To evolve, we had to learn to become love-givers, not just love-receivers.

We all know what happened then. We were cast out of the Garden and for the first time in our lives we felt shame, jealousy, anger, lack. We experienced highs and lows, joy and sorrow. Our lives became difficult. We had to work hard to survive. We had to make mistakes and learn from them.

Initially, we tried to blame others for our mistakes. But that did not make our lives any easier. It just deepened our pain and misery. We had to learn to face our fears, instead of projecting them onto each other.

Returning to the Garden, we are different than we were when we left hellbent on expressing our creativity at any cost. We return humble and sensitive to the needs of all. We return not just as created, but as co-creator, not just as son of man, but also as son of God."

Learn the Spiritual Practice
Associated with the Christ Mind Teachings

Living in the Heart The Affinity Process
and the Path of Unconditional Love
and Acceptance
Paperback $10.95
ISBN 1-879159-36-8
The long awaited, definitive book on the
Affinity Process is finally here. For years, the
Affinity Process has been refined by partici-
pants so that it could be easily understood
and experienced. Now, you can learn how to hold a safe, loving,
non-judgmental space for yourself and others which will enable
you to open your heart and move through your fears. The
Affinity Process will help you learn to take responsibility for your
fears and judgments so that you won't project them onto others. It will help you learn to listen deeply and without judgment
to others. And it will teach you how to tell your truth clearly
without blaming others for your experience.

Part One contains an in-depth description of the principles
on which the *Affinity Process* is based. Part Two contains a
detailed discussion of the *Affinity Group Guidelines.* And Part
Three contains a manual for people who wish to facilitate an
Affinity Group in their community.

If you are a serious student of the *Christ Mind* teachings, this
book is essential for you. It will enable you to begin a spiritual
practice which will transform your life and the lives of others. It
will also offer you a way of extending the teachings of love and
forgiveness throughout your community.

Now Finally our Bestselling Title on Audio Tape

Love Without Conditions,
Reflections of the Christ Mind, Part I
by Paul Ferrini
The Book on Tape Read by the Author
2 Cassettes, Approximately 3.25 hours
ISBN 1-879159-24-4 $19.95

Now on audio tape: the incredible book from Jesus calling us to awaken to our own Christhood. Listen to this gentle, profound book while driving in your car or before going to sleep at night. Elisabeth Kubler-Ross calls this "the most important book I have read. I study it like a Bible." Find out for yourself how this amazing book has helped thousands of people understand the radical teachings of Jesus and begin to integrate these teachings into their lives.

With its heartfelt combination of sensuality and spirituality, Paul Ferrini's poetry has been compared to the poetry of Rumi.

Crossing The Water: Poems About Healing and Forgiveness in Our Relationships

The time for healing and reconciliation has come, Ferrini writes. Our relationships help us heal childhood wounds, walk through our deepest fears, and cross over the water of our emotional pain. Just as the rocks in the river are pounded and caressed to rounded stone, the rough edges of our personalities are worn smooth in the context of a committed relationship. If we can keep our hearts open, we can heal together, experience genuine equality, and discover what it means to give and receive love without conditions.

With its heartfelt combination of sensuality and spirituality,

Paul Ferrini's poetry has been compared to the poetry of Rumi. These luminous poems demonstrate why Paul Ferrini is first a poet, a lover and a mystic. Come to this feast of the beloved with an open heart and open ears. 96 pp. paper. ISBN 1-879159-25-2 $9.95.

Miracle of Love: Reflections of the Christ Mind, Part III

In this volume of the Christ Mind series, Jesus sets the record straight regarding a number of events in his life. He tells us: "I was born to a simple woman in a barn. She was no more a virgin than your mother was." Moreover, the virgin birth was not the only myth surrounding his life and teaching. So were the concepts of vicarious atonement and physical resurrection.

Relentlessly, the master tears down the rigid dogma and hierarchical teachings that obscure his simple message of love and forgiveness. He encourages us to take him down from the pedestal and the cross and see him as an equal brother who found the way out of suffering by opening his heart totally. We too can open our hearts and find peace and happiness. "The power of love will make miracles in your life as wonderful as any attributed to me," he tells us. "Your birth into this embodiment is no less holy than mine. The love that you extend to others is no less important than the love I extend to you." 192 pp. paper ISBN 1-879159-23-6 $12.95.

The Ecstatic Moment: A Practical Manual for Opening Your Heart and Staying in It.

A simple, power-packed guide that helps us take appropriate responsibility for our experience and establish healthy boundaries with others. Part II contains many helpful exercises and meditations that teach us to stay centered, clear and open in heart and mind. The *Affinity Group Process* and other group practices help us learn important listening and communication skills that can transform our troubled relationships. Once you have read this book, you will keep it in your briefcase or on your bedside table, referring to it often. You will not find a more practical, down to earth guide to contemporary spirituality. You will want to order copies for all your friends. 128 pp. paper ISBN 1-879159-18-X $10.95

The Silence of the Heart: Reflections of the Christ Mind, Part II

A powerful sequel to *Love Without Conditions.* John Bradshaw says: "with deep insight and sparkling clarity, this book demonstrates that the roots of all abuse are to be found in our own self-betrayal. Paul Ferrini leads us skillfully and courageously beyond shame, blame, and attachment to our wounds into the depths of self-forgiveness . . . a must read for all people who are ready to take responsibility for their own healing." 218 pp. paper. ISBN 1-879159-16-3 $14.95

Love Without Conditions: Reflections of the Christ Mind, Part I

An incredible book calling us to awaken to our Christhood. Rarely has any book conveyed the teachings of the master in such a simple but profound manner. This book will help you to bring your understanding from the head to the heart so that you can model the teachings of love and forgiveness in your daily life. 192 pp. paper ISBN 1-879159-15-5 $12.00

The Wisdom of the Self

This ground-breaking book explores our authentic experience and our journey to wholeness. "Your life is your spiritual path. Don't be quick to abandon it for promises of bigger and better experiences. You are getting exactly the experiences you need to grow. If your growth seems too slow or uneventful for you, it is because you have not fully embraced the situations and relationships at hand . . . . To know the Self is to allow everything, to embrace the totality of who we are, all that we think and feel, all of our fear, all of our love." 229 pp. paper ISBN 1-879159-14-7 $12.00

The Twelve Steps of Forgiveness

A practical manual for healing ourselves and our relationships. This book gives us a step-by-step process for moving through our fears, projections, judgments, and guilt so that we can take responsibility for creating the life we want. With great gentleness, we learn to embrace our lessons and to find equality with others. 128 pp. paper ISBN 1-879159-10-4 $10.00

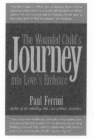

The Wounded Child's Journey: Into Love's Embrace

This book explores a healing process in which we confront our deep-seated guilt and fear, bringing love and forgiveness to the wounded child within. By surrendering our judgments of self and others, we overcome feelings of separation and dismantle co-dependent patterns that restrict our self-expression and ability to give and receive love. 225pp. paper ISBN 1-879159-06-6 $12.00

The Bridge to Reality

A Heart-Centered Approach to *A Course in Miracles* and the Process of Inner Healing. Sharing his experiences of spiritual awakening, Paul emphasizes self-acceptance and forgiveness as cornerstones of spiritual practice. Presented with beautiful photos, this book conveys the essence of The Course as it is lived in daily life. 192 pp. paper ISBN 1-879159-03-1 $12.00

Virtues of The Way

A lyrical work of contemporary scripture reminiscent of the *Tao Te Ching*. Beau-tifully illustrated, this inspirational book will help you cultivate the spiritual values required to fulfill your creative purpose and live in harmony with others. 64 pp. paper ISBN 1-879159-04-X $7.50

From Ego to Self

108 illustrated affirmations designed to offer you a new way of viewing conflict situations so that you can overcome negative thinking and bring more energy, faith and optimism into your life. 144 pp. paper ISBN 1-879159-01-5 $10.00

The Body of Truth

A crystal clear introduction to the universal teachings of love and forgiveness. This book traces all forms of suffering to negative attitudes and false beliefs, which we have the ability to transform. 64 pp. paper ISBN 1-879159-02-3 $7.50

Available Light

Inspirational, passionate poems dealing with the work of inner integration, love and relationships, death and re-birth, loss and abundance, life purpose and the reality of spiritual vision. 128 pp. paper ISBN 1-879159-05-8 $10.00

Poetry and Guided Meditation Tapes
by Paul Ferrini

The Poetry of the Soul

With its heartfelt combination of sensuality and spirituality, Paul Ferrini's poetry has been compared to the poetry of Rumi. These luminous poems read by the author demonstrate why Paul Ferrini is first a poet, a lover and a mystic. Come to this feast of the beloved with an open heart and open ears. With Suzi Kesler on piano. ISBN 1-879159-26-0 $10.00

The Circle of Healing

The meditation and healing tape that many of you have been seeking. This gentle meditation opens the heart to love's presence and extends that love to all the beings in your experience. A powerful tape with inspirational piano accompaniment by Michael Gray.
ISBN 1-879159-08-2 $10.00

Healing the Wounded Child

A potent healing tape that accesses old feelings of pain, fragmentation, self-judgment and separation and brings them into the light of conscious awareness and acceptance. Side two includes a hauntingly beautiful "inner child" reading from The Bridge to Reality with piano accompaniment by Michael Gray. ISBN 1-879159-11-2 $10.00

Forgiveness: Returning to the Original Blessing

A self healing tape that helps us accept and learn from the mistakes we have made in the past. By letting go of our judgments and ending our ego-based search for perfection, we can bring our darkness to the light, dissolving anger, guilt, and shame. Piano accompaniment by Michael Gray. ISBN 1-879159-12-0 $10.00

Paul Ferrini Talks and Workshop Tapes

Answering Our Own Call for Love

Paul tells the story of his own spiritual awakening: his Atheist upbringing, how he began to open to the presence of God, and his connection with Jesus and the Christ Mind teaching. In a very clear, heart-felt way, Paul presents to us the spiritual path of love, acceptance, and forgiveness. 1 Cassette ISBN 1-879159-33-4 $10.00

The Ecstatic Moment

Shows us how we can be with our pain compassionately and learn to nurture the light within ourselves, even when it appears that we are walking through darkness. Discusses subjects such as living in the present, acceptance, not fixing self or others, being with our discomfort and learning that we are lovable as we are. 1 Cassette ISBN 1-879159-27-3 $10.00

Honoring Self and Other

Helps us understand the importance of not betraying ourselves in our relationships with others. Focuses on understanding healthy boundaries, setting limits, and saying no to others in a loving way. Real life examples include a woman who is married to a man who is chronically critical of her, and a gay man who wants to tell his judgmental parents that he has AIDS. 1 Cassette ISBN 1-879159-34-1 $10.00

Seek First the Kingdom

Discusses the words of Jesus in the Sermon on the Mount: "Seek first the kingdom and all else will be added to you." Helps us understand how we create the inner temple by learning to hold our judgments of self and other more compassionately. The love of God flows through our love and acceptance of ourselves. As we establish our connection to the divine within ourselves, we don't need to look outside of ourselves for love and acceptance. Includes fabulous music by The Agape Choir and Band. 1 Cassette ISBN 1-879159-30-3 $10.00

Double Cassette Tape Sets

Ending the Betrayal of the Self

A roadmap for integrating the opposing voices in our psyche so that we can experience our own wholeness. Delineates what our responsibility is and isn't in our relationships with others, and helps us learn to set clear, firm, but loving boundaries. Our relationships can become areas of sharing and fulfillment, rather than mutual invitations to co-dependency and self betrayal. 2 Cassettes   ISBN 1-879159-28-7 $16.95

Relationships: Changing Past Patterns

Begins with a Christ Mind talk describing the link between learning to love and accept ourselves and learning to love and accept others. Helps us understand how we are invested in the past and continue to replay our old relationship stories. Helps us get clear on what we want and understand how to be faithful to it. By being totally committed to ourselves, we give birth to the beloved within and also without. Includes an in-depth discussion about meditation, awareness, hearing our inner voice, and the Affinity Group Process. 2 Cassettes ISBN 1-879159-32-5 $16.95

Relationship As a Spiritual Path

Explores concrete ways in which we can develop a relationship with ourselves and learn to take responsibility for our own experience, instead of blaming others for our perceived unworthiness. Also discussed: accepting our differences, the new paradigm of relationship, the myth of the perfect partner, telling our truth, compassion vs. rescuing, the unavailable partner, abandonment issues, negotiating needs, when to say no, when to stay and work on a relationship and when to leave. 2 Cassettes ISBN 1-879159-29-5 $16.95

Opening to Christ Consciousness

Begins with a Christ Mind talk giving us a clear picture of how the divine spark dwells within each of us and how we can open up to God-consciousness on a regular basis. Deals with letting go and forgiveness in our relationships with our parents, our children and our partners. A joyful, funny, and scintillating tape you will want to listen to many times. 2 Cassettes ISBN 1-879159-31-7 $16.95

Poster and Notecards

Risen Christ Posters & Notecards
11" x 17"
Poster suitable for framing
ISBN 1-879159-19-8 $10.00

Set of 8
Notecards with Envelopes
ISBN 1-879159-20-1 $10.00

Ecstatic Moment Posters & Notecards

8.5" x 11"
Poster suitable for framing
ISBN 1-879159-21-X $5.00

Set of 8 Notecards with Envelopes
ISBN 1-879159-22-8 $10.00

Heartways Press Order Form

Name _____

Address _____

City _____ State _____ Zip _____

Phone/Fax_____Email _____

Books by Paul Ferrini

The Living Christ ($14.95)   _____

Dancing with the Beloved ($12.95)   _____

The Great Way of All Beings:
   Renderings of Lao Tzu Hardcover ($23.00)   _____

Enlightenment for Everyone Hardcover ($16.00)   _____

Taking Back Our Schools ($10.95)   _____

The Way of Peace Hardcover ($19.95)   _____

   Way of Peace Dice ($3.00)   _____

Illuminations on the Road to Nowhere ($12.95)   _____

I am the Door Hardcover ($21.95)   _____

Reflections of the Christ Mind Hardcover ($19.95)   _____

Creating a Spiritual Relationship ($10.95)   _____

Grace Unfolding: Living a Surrendered Life ($9.95)   _____

Return to the Garden ($12.95)   _____

Living in the Heart ($10.95)   _____

Miracle of Love ($12.95)   _____

Crossing the Water ($9.95)   _____

The Ecstatic Moment ($10.95)   _____

The Silence of the Heart ($14.95)   _____

Love Without Conditions ($12.00)   _____

The Wisdom of the Self ($12.00)   _____

The Twelve Steps of Forgiveness ($10.00)   _____

The Circle of Atonement ($12.00)   _____

The Bridge to Reality ($12.00)   _____

From Ego to Self ($10.00)   _____

Virtues of the Way ($7.50)   _____

The Body of Truth ($7.50)   _____

Available Light ($10.00)   _____

Audio Tapes by Paul Ferrini

The Circle of Healing ($10.00) _____
Healing the Wounded Child ($10.00) _____
Forgiveness: The Original Blessing ($10.00) _____
The Poetry of the Soul ($10.00) _____
Seek First the Kingdom ($10.00) _____
Answering Our Own Call for Love ($10.00) _____
The Ecstatic Moment ($10.00) _____
Honoring Self and Other ($10.00) _____
Love Without Conditions ($19.95) 2 tapes _____
Ending the Betrayal of the Self ($16.95) 2 tapes _____
Relationships: Changing Past Patterns ($16.95) 2 tapes _____
Relationship As a Spiritual Path ($16.95) 2 tapes _____
Opening to Christ Consciousness ($16.95) 2 tapes _____

Posters and Notecards

Risen Christ Poster 11"x17" ($10.00) _____
Ecstatic Moment Poster 8.5"x11" ($5.00) _____
Risen Christ Notecards 8/pkg ($10.00) _____
Ecstatic Moment Notecards 8/pkg ($10.00) _____

Shipping

Priority Mail shipping for up to two items $3.95. _____
Add $1.00 for each additional item _____
Massachusetts residents please add 5% sales tax. _____
Add an extra $2.00 for shipping to Canada/Mexico _____
Add an extra $4.00 for shipping to Europe _____
Add an extra $6.00 for shipping to other countries _____
TOTAL _____

Send Order To: Heartways Press P. O. Box 99,
Greenfield, MA 01302-0099   413-774-9474
Toll free: 1-888-HARTWAY (Orders only)
www.paulferrini.com
www.heartwayspresss.com
email: heartway@crocker.com